Chesapeake Bay Notes & Sketches

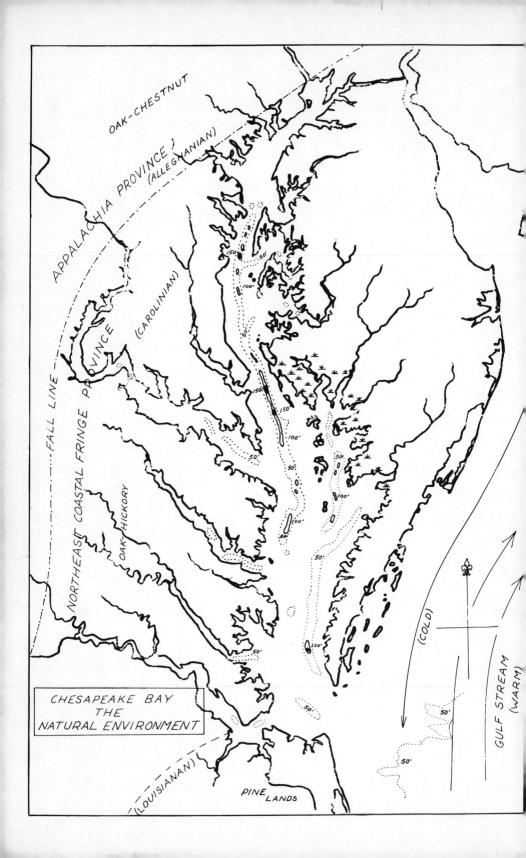

OAK-CHESTNUT

APPALACHIA PROVINCE
(ALLEGHANIAN)

FALL LINE

(CAROLINIAN)

NORTHEAST COASTAL FRINGE PROVINCE

OAK-HICKORY

150
50
100

150

150

100'

50'

50'

0

50'

100'

0

50'

100'

0'

50'

100'

50'

50'

100'

50'

50'

CHESAPEAKE BAY
THE
NATURAL ENVIRONMENT

(LOUISIANAN)

PINE LANDS

(COLD)

GULF STREAM (WARM)

50'

50'

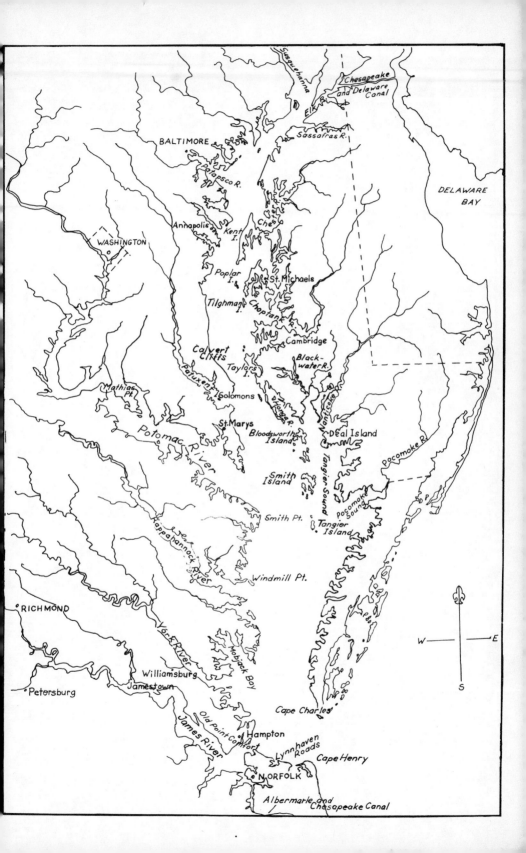

Susquehanna

Chesapeake
and Delaware
Canal

ELK R.

Sassafras R.

BALTIMORE

Patapsco R.

DELAWARE
BAY

Annapolis

Kent
I.

Ches.

WASHINGTON

Poplar
I.

St. Michaels

Tilghman I.

Choptank R.

Calvert
Cliffs

Cambridge

Taylors I.

Black-
water R.

Patuxent R.

Solomons

Mathias
Pt.

Honga R.

St. Marys

Bloodsworth
Island

Deal Island

Potomac River

Wicomico R.

Nanticoke R.

Pocomoke R.

Smith
Island

Tangier Sound

P.

Smith Pt.

Pocomoke
Sound

Rappahannock River

Tangier
Island

Windmill Pt.

RICHMOND

York River

W — E

Mobjack Bay

Williamsburg

S

Petersburg

Jamestown

Old Point Comfort

Cape Charles

James River

Hampton

Lynnhaven
Roads

Cape Henry

NORFOLK

Albermarle and
Chesapeake Canal

Chesapeake Bay Notes & Sketches

Carvel Hall Blair
and
Willits Dyer Ansel

TIDEWATER PUBLISHERS
Centreville, Maryland

ISBN 0-87033-277-5

Library of Congress Catalog Card Number: 76-124311

Manufactured in the United States of America
First edition, 1970; First paperback edition, 1981

*This book is dedicated
to our children*

Contents

Introduction

IT IS NOT difficult to imagine how the finest of the world's estuaries, Chesapeake Bay, looked to the first Englishmen who came to settle and use it three hundred and fifty years ago. It is not difficult because many left accurate descriptions and because, most fortunately, Chesapeake Bay remains relatively unspoiled. Many of its creeks and bays still seem remote when one explores them today. The Chesapeake impresses us with its beauty as it impressed those first Europeans who sailed it and wrote of it.

> *"The north Cape is called Cape Charles in honor of the worthy Duke of York. Within is a country that may have the prerogative over the most pleasant places of Europe, Asia, Africa, or America, for better and pleasant navigable rivers: heaven and earth never agreed better to frame a place for man's habitation. . . . Here are mountains, hills, plains, valleys, rivers, and brooks all running most pleasantly into a fair bay compassed but for the mouth with fruitful and delightful land. In the Bay and rivers are many isles both great and small, some woody, some plaine, and most of them low and not inhabited."*
>
> ### Captain John Smith

The marshes John Smith described and the points he named are still there. The shores are covered with the same kinds of trees; the insects that plagued him are still a nuisance. Most of the birds and fish he noted are still found in the Bay, but not in the numbers he recorded. The animal life on the shore has changed, and the Indians, whose customs and language Smith took pains to describe, have almost completely disappeared.

Lord Baltimore's people wrote of the conditions and resources of the Proprietor's colony, Maryland. They wrote of the plentiful fish and fowl, of the rich land with unlimited promise and wealth, blessed by a healthy, temperate climate. One purpose of their writing was to attract colonists to the new land, but their awe of the beauty and richness of the country was sincere. This awareness of limitless opportunity in a virgin land was to dominate American imaginations for three hundred years. Calvert was not the first, nor was he to be the last, to attempt to build a new and better society in America.

After three hundred years of exploiting, the American is forced to face the reality that the resources can be exhausted, the country become crowded, and the beautiful land spoiled. Today the Chesapeake is still beautiful and largely unspoiled, but it is threatened.

Population projections anticipate seven and one half million people will inhabit the Washington-Baltimore metropolitan complex by 1985. A megalopolis will flank the Bay's Western Shore, a vast strip of heavily populated suburbs. An industrialized society such as ours places extraordinary demands on the natural environment. Man's triumph has been his ability to change and control the environment. Pollution on a tremendous scale manifested in a multitude of ways has been the by-product of this progress.

It is because we share the admiration of Smith and others and because we are concerned for the future of the Chesapeake that we are attempting this description of it, the story of man's use of it, and the factors and conditions that threaten it.

C. H. B.

W. D. A.

Chesapeake Bay Notes & Sketches

I

Geology and Geography

FOR 35 MILES, from Drum Point north to Fishing Creek, the Calvert Cliffs edge the western shore of Chesapeake Bay. The long unbroken bluff contrasts sharply with the low-lying shores, indented with innumerable river and creek mouths, that line the rest of the Bay. A hiker on the strand at the foot of the Cliffs looks up at strata upon strata of silt and fossils laid down some 15 million years ago. Giant scallop shells stand out in the escarpment and sharks' teeth lie in the rubble underfoot. The Cliffs form the edge of a section of what was once the bottom of the Bay, uplifted over the millenniums and finally thrust as high as 190 feet above the water's edge. In the early morning one need share the scene only with the towhees and yellowthroats that dart about the foliage overhanging the cliff edge and choking crevices in its wall. The sun, low over the Eastern Shore, burns through the haze and reflects from the flat, oil-calm water. The solitude of the Cliffs is accentuated by an awareness of their age. Man—his works and his problems—seem insignificant.

A small museum at Scientist's Cliffs displays a collection of fossils. A placard reads:

> During the Miocene Period—10 to 15 million years ago—the Maryland coast probably resembled the present Georgia, Florida, and Gulf of Mexico coasts. It was a region of dunes, lagoons, and shallow seas, protected from the open ocean by a barrier reef. Temperatures were from ten to 15 degrees warmer than today. Turtles and crocodiles lived in the lagoons and in the sea.

The Calvert Cliffs contain the world's largest accessible deposits of Miocene fossils. Over the years they have been the subject of over 500 scientific papers by geologists and paleontologists. The Maryland Academy of Sciences and the Smithsonian Institution are continuing these investigations at the construction site of the Baltimore Gas and Electric Company's nuclear plant above Cove Point. Excavation of one million cubic

1

feet of earth is revealing myriads of fossils, including three previously unknown species, two gastropods and one clam.

Layers of Pleistocene, Miocene, and Eocene deposits may be seen in the
cliff walls. These are found in twenty-three distinct zones. The Miocene
deposits, early, middle, and late, have been given the Maryland names
Calvert, Choptank, and St. Marys. The fossil record of the life of the
Miocene period is clear in the Cliffs. Land mammals are represented by

Miocene Deposits

the dog, horse, peccary, mastodon, tapir, and rhinoceros. The Cliffs are
also rich in Miocene marine mammals. Twenty-two species of whale, seal,
and porpoise are present. Some four hundred species of mollusk fossils are
densely packed into beds over a foot thick. Shark and ray fossils are
plentiful. Certain species of bony fish found in the Bay today were living
in the shallow seas fifteen million years ago. Croakers, weakfish, catfish,
drum, sailfish, and sunfish swam those waters. The bird population has
not so greatly changed from the Miocene period. Gulls, shearwaters,
gannets, loons, and cormorants fished or scavenged then as now.

Since the Miocene period, the Bay country has been alternately submerged and exposed as the glaciers' advance and retreat caused the rise
and fall of the ocean. For periods a thousand years in length the coastal
plain as far as the Piedmont was flooded by salt water. At other times the

level of the sea was almost five hundred feet below its present height and
the coastal plain was dry out to what are now the limits of the continental
shelf. The Bay as we know it is fairly young; it took its present rough
outlines as recently as ten thousand years ago.

The Bay, of course, is still changing. In the present interglacial period
the earth's ice caps are melting and the oceans are slowly rising causing

Miocene Fossils

the Chesapeake to grow in size. More important, from our limited per-
spective, waves, currents, tides, weathering, and erosion cause changes
discernible to a man in his lifetime. Winter storms pound the sandy shores
of the Chesapeake and quickly wash them away. Poplar Island, off Tilghman Island on the Eastern Shore, is eroding rapidly. In the 17th century
the island measured about one thousand acres. Sixty years ago it was
half that size; now it is only one hundred acres and has been cut in three
pieces. Northwest winds drive waves against its shores, bringing banks
and pines down together. The Smithsonian Institution, owner of the
diminishing island, is trying to save it as a nesting place for birds. All told
Maryland lost about 6,000 acres in the century between the 1840s and the
1940s. Erosion rates vary, depending upon configuration of the coast,
patterns of currents, exposure to weather, and composition of the soil. The
eroded soil is displaced only a short distance into deeper water; as a

result the shoulders of the Bay are sandy while the midchannels have bottoms of clay and silt carried down by the rivers. Erosion is most severe on the Eastern Shore between the Choptank River and the Honga River. Here, more than half an acre per mile of shore each year is lost.

Sharp's Island is another example of erosion on the Eastern Shore. In colonial times the island was a rich plantation of six hundred acres, separated from Tilghman Island by a channel so narrow that a colonial governor swam his horse across it. Now the island is gone; a light marks a shallow spot still charted as Sharp's Island. Tilghman Island too has receded. Today the governor would have to swim his horse over two miles of open water fifteen to twenty feet deep. The island went quickly; within living memory it was the site of a white frame hotel. Kent Island is losing valuable farm land, and its landowners build bulkheads and appeal to

Western Shore in Calvert County

the state for help. Lower in the Bay, Hooper Island is cut by two channels and seems to be fated to be washed away.

The Western Shore too is eroding. People on the Northern Neck in Virginia have moved summer houses two and three times back from the shore. Across the Potomac on Point Lookout, erosion has claimed a fifty acre field along with two Civil War earthwork forts. Up the Potomac on the Maryland side, St. Clements, or Blackistone Island, is one-tenth as large as the settlers found it in 1634. Preventing erosion with bulkheads or jetties is expensive and not always successful. In Maryland, the state will share the cost, but 2,000 miles of shore need protection. St. Clements Island illustrates the difficulties. Between 1964 and 1966, one hundred thousand dollars' worth of stone was placed along its shore. It is now apparent that the work was to no effect and erosion continues.

The waters of the Atlantic once covered the coastal plain west to what is now the fall line. This is the head of navigation of the broad rivers of the plain, where the first falls or rapids mark the beginning of the Piedmont Plateau. The rivers below, as arms of the ocean, are subject to the tides.

Western Shore Creek

At the southern end of the Bay, the Tidewater belt extends inland some fifty miles. It narrows on the upper Western Shores until, at the head of the Chesapeake, the Susquehanna's rapids lie within sight of the Bay. Here the foothills of the Appalachians reach the water, and high headlands line the shore. The view from Havre de Grace across to Elk Neck is reminiscent of New England. Elk Neck, like the Calvert Cliffs, stands in sharp contrast to the rest of the Chesapeake's low shores.

The Chesapeake is the drowned river valley of the Susquehanna, a shallow pan creased by a narrow channel. The mean depth of the Bay is only a little over 27½ feet; the maximum depth of the channel is a hole 180 feet deep. The surface area of the Chesapeake is 2,320 square miles. Besides the Bay itself, 50 major tributaries and countless minor ones add an additional 2,120 square miles of water surface. The result is 1,750 miles of navigable waterway in the Tidewater and 4,600 miles of shoreline. Completing the estuarine system is the land which it drains, in the case of the Chesapeake, some 64,000 square miles along the Eastern and Western Shores.

The earliest accurate chart and geography of the Bay were the work of Captain John Smith. His voyage to the head of the Chesapeake in 1608 resulted in *Smith's Description of Virginia*, a survey which included a remarkably precise chart. Smith left his base at Jamestown and sailed north, exploring and describing the navigable rivers as he went. He noted the navigable James, York, Rappahannock, Potomac, Patuxent, and then—omitting West River, South River, Severn, and Magothy—the Patapsco. Smith also missed a few rivers including the Chester and the Choptank, on the Eastern Shore, but his north-south distances are very accurate. On his map, dividers measure 53½ leagues, 160 miles, from Cape Henry to what is now Havre de Grace. Today's chart makes the distance 157 miles. From Old Point Comfort at the mouth of the James to Point Lookout at the mouth of the Potomac, a modern chart shows 63 miles; Smith measured 66. His east-west distances are less accurate; the early chart shows the lower narrows of the Bay at Wolf Trap seven miles across; the actual distance is twelve. From Cape Charles to Hampton Roads, Smith plotted twenty-three miles, four miles too great. The 17th century

West River in Maryland

navigator could measure meridian altitudes of celestial bodies with the astrolabes or cross staffs then available; from there he determined latitudes and north-south distances. East-west measurements, on the other hand, are a function of longitude and one can find longitude only if he knows the precise time. Smith lived before the invention of the marine chronometer, and was forced to estimate east-west distances by dead reckoning or by seaman's eye. He still produced excellent results. A modern yachtsman, using Smith's chart, could safely pilot from the Susquehanna to Richmond, or from Washington to the Virginia Capes.

The soil of the Tidewater is different from that of the Piedmont. Once a sea bottom, Tidewater soils are sandy with few rocks, composed of clays, silts, and subordinate gravels. The rock of the coastal plain is sedimentary; that of the foothills is hard and crystalline. The soil of the Tidewater quickly loses its fertility. Organic matter and humus are quickly oxidized, while the minerals, plant foods, are leached away when the soil is broken for planting. It erodes easily, and silt from the old fields fills the broad, slow-moving rivers.

As the shores of the Bay have been receding, the rivers and creeks have been filling with sediment brought down from the watershed area drained by the tributaries. Geologists estimate that waterborne sediment now is from four to eight times the amount carried before the coming of the English. Agriculture and, more recently, clearing for the building associated with increasing urbanization account for the ever-increasing sedi-

Knapps Narrows

mentation. Many towns built at the head of navigation are now well above it. Others are still seaports only because of constant dredging. In colonial times Port Tobacco, Hartford-on-the-Bush, Joppa Town, and Upper Marlboro were ports. Shipping reaches them no longer; Upper Marlboro, for example, is eight miles above navigable waters. Sedimentation of ports was a problem even in colonial days. Dredging began as early as 1804 to keep the Potomac open to Georgetown. Without continuous dredging, the head of navigation would be twenty miles below Washington today. In Baltimore harbor, more than fifteen feet of sediment has settled to the bottom in the last hundred years. Sedimentation, and the question of where to dump the output of the dredges, will become an increasing problem as new construction produces even greater erosion.

The Delmarva Peninsula forms the eastern margin of the coastal plain. Its Chesapeake shore consists of low banks a few feet above sea level bordered by a series of islands, some in the making, some disappearing.

Kent, Tilghman, Taylors, Hooper, Bloodsworth, Smith and Tangier Islands are separated by wide, shallow bays and sounds: Eastern, Fishing, Tangier, and Pocomoke. Narrows and creeks divide them from the Eastern Shore proper. Tidal rivers—the Sassafras, Chester, Miles, Choptank, Nanticoke, and Pocomoke—enter the bays and sounds. The ebb and flood of the tides reach upriver to the center of the Peninsula.

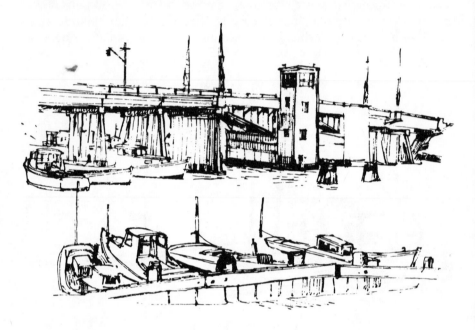

Kent Island Narrows

At the southern end of the Eastern Shore the land is even lower and finally merges with the Bay in great salt marshes. Marshes are found at the heads of creeks throughout the Bay, but the southern wetlands are far more extensive. Thousands of acres, cut by meandering channels, lie below the Choptank in Dorchester County. Clumps of loblolly pine on the solid hillocks give the appearance of headlands breaking the straight line of the horizon. Various grasses with high salt tolerance and thickly tangled root systems maintain the turf. Though salt water covers the marsh at high tide, it does not penetrate the impervious peaty ground. The dominant marsh grasses prevent the succession of other plants, and maintain a state of constancy in the marsh.

Few men visit the marshes except the hunter, trapper, and waterman. Scattered settlements supported by oystering, clamming, and crabbing are gradually dying. The marshes belong to the mosquito, sweat fly, muskrat, and, in spring and fall, the waterfowl. Above the endless flat expanse of marsh the sky is infinitely clear and clean. Small in the distance

Maryland Marsh

a hawk rises from a weathered pine snag to hover high above the brown grasses and add to the impression of great space. Invaluable for their wildlife, the salt marshes are the most remote and unchanging parts of the Bay region.

Miocene Deposits at Calvert Cliffs

II

Chesapeake Weather and Climate

TECHNICALLY SPEAKING, the Bay's climate is termed humid subtropical; that is, it is warm, temperate, and rainy. The factors that produce these conditions in the Chesapeake are the same that affect climate everywhere, the amount of sunlight, distribution of land and water masses, and the presence of high and low pressure areas. The Chesapeake is between the Gulf Stream in the Atlantic to the east and the North American continental land mass to the west. To seaward, the Azores High, a semipermanent high pressure area, influences Chesapeake weather as it makes its seasonal migrations. The sum of these factors is an average temperature in the coldest month of 27 degrees Fahrenheit, roughly the southern limit of frozen ground and snow cover. The average temperature of the warmest month is 72 degrees. There is no dry season. The driest month receives, on the average, at least 1.2 inches of rain. The conditions at both ends of the Bay, at Norfolk and Baltimore, are within the limits of subtropical conditions. From the human point of view, it is a pleasant climate.

Baltimore, farther inland and less subject to the moderating influence of the Atlantic, is colder in midwinter than Norfolk. Although mean January temperatures are above 32 degrees, some winters are considerably colder with long spells of freezing weather. At such times the Bay freezes hard, which is unusual. Creeks in the northern end of the Bay freeze almost every winter, but ice on the James at the southern end is rare.

Ice is a problem to the oystermen; in years past they have been driven to cutting slots through the ice over the bars and dragging the dredges by hand through the cuts. During the winter of 1967-1968, the tonging boats were frozen in, the price of oysters rose, and at last the oystermen in one town smashed their way to the beds in an old landing barge pressed into service as an icebreaker. The small boats of the Bay, the deadrises and Hooper Islanders, are sometimes sheathed in copper; the sheathing forward is carried higher for work in the ice. Sometimes they are helped in the fight to keep the creeks open by the boats of the Coast Guard and the

11

Department of Natural Resources in Maryland. Old-timers among the Bay watermen tell of Eastern Shore farmers crossing to Baltimore by sled. Today the main ship channel to Baltimore is never closed to oceangoing vessels; the passing of large numbers of these steel-hulled ships keeps the channel open. Baltimore harbor itself must sometimes be cleared by city-maintained icebreakers. A few iceboats have sailed the Bay. One is in the Chesapeake Bay Maritime Museum at St. Michaels, and there are pictures of others carrying rigs like those of the crab scrapers of the summer months.

The Middle of the Chesapeake

At the other extreme of climate, the Chesapeake can get very hot. The hottest month is July; the water is warmest, however, in August, averaging a tepid 80 degrees. Summer is a time of many calms when in the middle of the Bay the air dies while the sun glares unmercifully off the water. At such times the flies always seem to find one's boat, even several miles from the nearest shore. The wash from merchant vessels bound to or from Baltimore travels for miles across the glassy calm. If one happens to lie helpless and becalmed in the track of the ships, one sweats even more than the humidity warrants for the ships, rising huge and menacing, seem bent on running one down. As the ships pass, the sound of the bow wave and machinery rolls across the water. The boom swings wildly and gear slides and rattles as the wash hits. The flies rise for a moment and then settle again to resume their stinging and buzzing.

On such days there may be optical illusions. The distortion is vertical; sails of boats tower in the sky; low bluffs on shore shoot up forming vertical columns and impressive cliffs. The tall forms then become hazy and less solid; they separate and then reform at the base at the proper height. Lighthouses become very tall and, at times, seem to detach at the bottom. Headlands float above the horizon, where the water is the same bright, glassy grey as the sky above. It is difficult to decide where water ends and sky begins.

The prevailing winds of the Chesapeake result from airflow around the Azores and continental pressure cells. In winter the pressure over North

America is high. The Azores High has moved eastward and has relatively less effect. Under these conditions, the continental winds dominate and come chiefly from the north. The mean wind at Norfolk in January and February is from north-northeast at ten knots. In summer, the Azores High has expanded into the western Atlantic, while the continental land mass, heated by the long summer days, has become the center of a cell of low pressure. Now both cells tend to cause a flow of air from the south over the Bay; Norfolk's mean winds are southerly from April through August, with minimum velocity, averaging seven knots, in July.

Average statistics may be misleading, for the Bay lies in an area where extremes are as common as means. Summer thunderstorms are frequent, approaching ten per month in July. Local conditions often dominate. Winds flowing up or down the Bay are steady; offshore winds are generally gusty. Northerlies or southerlies, especially after days of blowing, build up a steep, choppy sea in the shallow waters of the Chesapeake. Offshore breezes lack the fetch, and the sea is flatter. Brief, squally catspaws are frequent with the wind from the west. In the summer, the middle of the day is often airless and still, unless the breeze is coming steadily up the Chesapeake from the south. Early in the day or in the late afternoon there is some stirring of the air.

Fall provides the best sailing weather. A breeze is certain, the water is clear and cold, and the air is brisk, a refreshing contrast to the torpor of the hot, calm summer. A wind blowing steadily up the Bay makes for strenuous sailing in a small boat. The spray drives over the weather bow and glitters in the bright, fall sun; varnished wood and white paintwork shine, and water streams off raingear. The crew, togged out in rain clothes and gloves, hike out over the cold water rushing along the weather side. With the wind on the quarter, the boat planes on the top of crests giving the impression of great speed. At other times, the seas rise astern; the boat seems caught permanently in the trough with a moving crest of water before and behind. Ahead of a crest, she hangs canted downward for minutes on a slope as boat and sea fall together into the trough. Summer visitors have gone; one shares the Bay with the waterfowl. Topping the crests, one sees large flocks of ducks flying along the troughs. Geese and swans take to wing, calling as they fly. Autumn sails on the Bay leave vivid memories.

Southerly winds reach the Bay after absorbing moisture from the Gulf of Mexico; they make summers rainier than winters. In Baltimore, August is normally the wettest month with 4.4 inches of rain; November and December are driest with 3.0 inches. Fogs occur throughout the year, somewhat more frequently in the lower Bay.

Conditions are most changeable in the summer. An airless calm can give way to a thirty-knot line squall. Typically, one is adrift in mid-Bay, becalmed. Thunder to the northwest is the first clue, and one rouses to see a dark sky over the Western Shore. A westerly breeze picks up and the temperature falls. The sky darkens quickly, a threatening bluish slate to windward, an unhealthy yellowish to leeward. Lightning flashes in the quarter of the approaching storm, but the sun continues to shine from the west, throwing an intense, strong light. Sails shine unnaturally white, and the water takes on a strong greyish blue. After a sudden, cold gust, the rain strikes, and the shore and other boats disappear in the hard, driving rain.

The wise sailor douses his sails promptly and has little to do but watch and shiver in the cold. The splashing of the rain, the wind, and the thunder join in a general uproar. The squall reaches a climax when hail strikes. Marble-sized stones come rattling down, rolling and bouncing across floorboards and deck. Thunder and flapping sails add to the din. Suddenly the storm blows over. The air is now much colder than the water and a low mist rises from the surface to a level of six feet. Standing to see over it, one watches the Western Shore reemerge in brilliant sun while the Eastern Shore takes the brunt of the squall. Bay weather is up to form; "If you don't like it, just wait."

III

The Early Years — Calvert versus Claiborne

A MARYLAND PRIEST, writing in the 1630s, compared the sisters Leah and Rachel to Virginia and her younger sister colony, Maryland. Conditions in the two colonies were remarkably similar, and the presence and experience of Virginia undoubtedly aided the settling of Maryland. Rather than friendship, however, suspicion and rivalry marked the sisters' relations. The theme of Maryland's early years was a bitter feud between William Claiborne of Virginia and the Calverts of Maryland.

The Irish peer George Calvert, the first Lord Baltimore, entered the New World with a colony in Newfoundland. Discouraged by the harsh climate, Lord Baltimore abandoned the colony and coasted south to more temperate regions. A former member of the Virginia Company, he inspected Delaware Bay and, entering the Chesapeake, called in 1629 at Jamestown. The visit of a rival colonist proved unwelcome. When one of the Virginians threatened to strike him, the authorities pilloried the belligerent settler for insulting a nobleman. Simultaneously they contrived to get rid of him, demanding that Baltimore swear an oath of allegiance and supremacy. A loyal Catholic, Baltimore refused and returned to England. So began a tug of war in which control of Maryland changed hands half a dozen times over the next thirty years.

Leader of the anti-Calvert Virginians was William Claiborne. Since his arrival in 1621 he had served energetically and ably in the affairs of the colony. Particularly interested in the Eastern Shore and the upper Bay, he traded with the Indians and established settlements on Kent Island and at the mouth of the Susquehanna. He claimed the title of gentleman proprietor of Kent Island. Divining correctly that Baltimore's interest in the Bay would not cease after his quick survey, Claiborne hastened after him to England. His suspicions were well founded. Calvert had applied for a proprietorship within the Virginia grant, first for lands south of the James and then for territory to the north. Claiborne guarded his interests in the upper Bay by bringing to bear his own influence in court, but he

15

was no match for Calvert. Charles I promised a charter giving Maryland to Baltimore. The fortieth parallel was to become the southern boundary on the Eastern Shore, as charted on John Smith's map, to the Atlantic. Across the Bay, the boundary was to run:

> Unto the true meridian of the first fountain of the river of the Pattowmack, thence verging toward the South, unto the further bank of the said river, and following the same on the West and South, unto a certain place called Cinquack, and situate near the north of the said river, where it disembogues into the aforesaid bay of Chesapeake.

Lord Baltimore's experience in Newfoundland had familiarized him with royal charters. In his second venture he took care to obtain sovereignty over the entire Potomac River, rather than sharing it with Virginia. To

Calvert Cliffs

this day Maryland holds title over the river not merely to the middle but all the way to the low-water mark on the southern shore. Over the years the location of the boundary has had interesting consequences. In 1785, for example, a question over navigation of the Potomac gave rise to a conference in Annapolis on relations between the states. This convention led directly to the Philadelphia Convention which drafted the Federal Constitution. More recently the boundary line permitted Maryland gambling interests to invade Virginia. Slot machine operators took advantage of piers extending into the river from the Virginia shore. Virginians, legally barred from gambling in their own state, could enter Maryland merely by walking a few steps along the pier. At the pier head, where Maryland laws prevailed, slot machines whirled busily and legally.

The first Lord Baltimore did not see Maryland again nor did he live to receive the charter. Shortly after his death, the patent was arranged and went to his eldest son and heir, Cecilius Calvert, the Second Baron Baltimore. Cecil Calvert ruled the colony as a lord proprietor, but remained himself in England. Under his sponsorship some 200 colonists landed from the *Ark* and the *Dove* at St. Marys in 1634. The lord proprietor's brother Leonard Calvert served as governor.

Claiborne, first on the ground with his colony at Kent Island, continued to protest, but the Calverts' charter was upheld on the grounds that Claiborne held only a trading license. Not one to give in easily, Claiborne took matters into his own hands by stirring up Indian troubles. The settlers initially had found the Indians friendly. The situation changed, as related by the Jesuit, Very Reverend Father Matins Vitellestis:

> The Governor [Calvert] had taken with him as a companion, on his voyage to the Emperor [the Indian Chief] Henry Fleet, a captain from the Virginia colony, a man especially acceptable to the Savages, well versed in their language, and acquainted with the country. This man was, at first, very intimate with us, afterwards, being misled by the evil councils of one Clayborne, he became very hostile to us, and excited the natives to anger against us by all the means in his power.

Although hostile Indians did not destroy the colony, Lord Baltimore feared that it would be "overthrowne now in the infancy of it." He instructed his brother Leonard to seize Claiborne and take possession of Kent Island. The Marylanders intercepted one of Claiborne's boats, the pinnace *Long Tail* bound up the Bay to Kent Island, and captured it. In retaliation Claiborne fitted out an armed boat, placed one Lieutenant Warren in charge, and ordered the capture of any vessels from St. Marys. Calvert expanded his navy by two armed pinnaces, *St. Margaret* and *St. Helen,* under the command of a Captain Cornwallis. The rival boats met in Pocomoke Sound in April, 1635, on the border line on the Eastern Shore, and fought the first naval battle of the Chesapeake. Claiborne's men fired first, killing one man aboard the Maryland boats. The return fire killed Lieutenant Warren and two of his Virginians. The engagement ended, but not the feud.

Claiborne's friends rallied to his defense. Governor Harvey of Virginia had tried to maintain good relations with the Calverts. The Virginians sent him home. The Maryland government attempted to extradite Claiborne to try him for piracy, but with the governor gone they were thwarted. Claiborne for his part returned to England to petition the king and failed again to shake the Calverts' charter. In the meantime Maryland, through a bill of attainder, confiscated all his property and convicted one of his lieutenants of piracy.

Back in Virginia, the doughty Claiborne nursed his grievances and conspired with his Kent Islanders. Events in England gave him his chance with the triumph of the Parliamentary Party. As a supporter of the king, Baltimore's power waned. Claiborne exploited the disaffection of the Maryland Puritans and, with the help of the Kent Islanders, led a rebellion against Governor Leonard Calvert. The governor had most of the advantages; his policies and those of the lord proprietor had been eminently reasonable and he enjoyed strong popular support. Claiborne nevertheless succeeded in replacing the governor and taking power himself. Vengeful and harsh, he expelled the Jesuits and sent Father White, historian of the colony, home in chains to England. The economy faltered and the colony languished. Across the Atlantic Lord Baltimore lost hope of recovering his colony, but his brother, in exile in Virginia under the protection of Governor Berkeley, was more sanguine. He returned to St. Marys with a small force and received the welcome of the people. Kent Island capitulated after threat of invasion and blockade, and Calvert regained the governorship. The Maryland Assembly passed a second bill of attainder and laid the death penalty and confiscation of all property on anyone supporting Claiborne. The Virginian was not discouraged; he continued to claim Kent Island, threatened and defied the governor, and waited for more political changes in England. When Cromwell became Lord Protector of England in 1653, Claiborne left the Anglicans and attached himself to the Puritan cause. Lord Baltimore followed suit, but not fast enough, and lost his proprietorship of Maryland. The government appointed a commission to manage the colony, with Claiborne among the commissioners.

The Puritans controlled Maryland for six years, repealed Calvert's liberal religious Toleration Act, and on the Severn River repelled a military attempt to restore Baltimore to power. Politics in England again intervened to change the government in Maryland. In 1658 Baltimore made up with Cromwell and was allowed to appoint a new governor. Three years later a fourth Calvert, Cecil's son Charles, assumed the governorship and in 1675 succeeded to his father's baronetcy and to the proprietorship of the colony. Claiborne's struggle with the Calverts ended in failure, but not before he had tried every trick of politics, commerce, and war on both sides of the Atlantic. Seventeenth century gentlemen adventurers played for high stakes, and they played the game to the bitter end.

IV

Battle of the Severn—1655

SPA CREEK joins the Severn River two and one half miles west of Tolly Point and the Bay. Upriver from the confluence lies Annapolis; downriver Eastport spreads inland from the shores of Horn Point. Once a sleepy Bay village of cottages and boatyards, Eastport now boasts high-rise apartment houses with elevator service from yacht float to luxurious suites. Three centuries ago, before even the village existed, the woods of Horn Point were a bloody battlefield where colonist fought colonist in an extension of seventeenth century England's internal conflicts. Not content to subdue a wilderness, the early Americans had energy to spare for an impressive amount of legal, political, and religious squabbling. Passions ran high; godly and rational men, usurping power by force of arms, killed each other in open battle or execution by firing squad after a drumhead trial.

The circumstances that led to the engagement were complicated; so were the tactics of the battle itself and its aftermath. The trouble began in 1649 when the Puritans beheaded Charles I at Whitehall. In England, Lord Baltimore had tried to be equally accommodating to Crown, Parliament, Anglican, Catholic, and Protestant. In America he had welcomed Puritans to his colony, even refugees from the persecution of Anglican Governor Berkeley in Virginia. Three hundred "Roundheads" had fled from the intolerant Anglicans of the Old Dominion to a generous tract granted them by Calvert at Providence on the Severn. Free land, equal civil rights, and religious tolerance notwithstanding, the Puritans returned Baltimore's consideration with hostility and ingratitude. It was at this juncture that word of the king's death reached the acting governor of Maryland. Less astute than Governor Stone, his deputy misjudged the political atmosphere in the colony and in England by proclaiming his loyalty to Charles II, son of the beheaded monarch. The Puritan Parliament, reacting in London, decreed royalist Maryland to be in a state of rebellion. So encouraged, the Maryland Roundheads deposed the acting governor and assumed power. Baltimore hastily repudiated his agent's declaration for Charles II and dispatched Governor Stone back to the Chesapeake to reassert the propri-

19

etor's authority. Lord Protector Cromwell was disposed to be tolerant of Catholics in faraway Maryland, though he dealt with them harshly enough in nearby Ireland. He decided to back Stone and Baltimore rather than the American Roundheads, evidently preferring to support law and order rather than ideology. Thus the stage was set for the Battle of the Severn: insurgent Puritans in control of the colonial government pitted against the deposed governor with the backing of the English government.

Stone marshalled his hundred and thirty men in St. Marys and moved against the center of resistance at Providence. His force came up the Western Shore in a dozen small unarmed boats. At Herring Bay he received two messengers from the rebels offering to parley, but he took them prisoner and pushed on without replying. Roundheads in Providence mobilized one hundred and fifty men and secured the services of two armed vessels, the *Golden Lion* and a smaller vessel of two guns.

Anne Arundel County Creek

The governor's forces proceeded around Tolly Point into the Severn and headed toward the Roundhead vessels anchored in the inner harbor at Providence. As the governor's flotilla bore down, the Puritans challenged and warned the boats off first with a warning shot and then an aimed one. After a shouted exchange Stone sheered off and headed for a creek, one assumes Spa Creek, and landed on Horn Point. The Roundhead ships followed and took position to prevent Stone from re-embarking to put to sea again.

The Marylanders, as the Puritans called Governor Stone's men, were in a difficult tactical position. Presumably they had not calculated on the

Roundhead naval power. Blockaded on Horn Point with no place to march, they considered their dilemma. The governor decided on a military demonstration on the shore: flying of banners, beating of drums, playing of martial music, and shouting at the ships:

"Come ye rogues! Come ye rogues! Roundhead Dogs!"

This display provoked a shot from the ships which killed one man, and the governor's men took cover in the woods. They prepared fireships for use that night to break the blockade.

The Roundheads were not ones to tarry. While the ships occupied the St. Marys men to seaward, a landing force rowed up the Severn, went ashore and marched six miles around the headwaters of Spa Creek to take the enemy in the rear. The Roundhead cry as they fell on their surprised enemy was:

"In the name of God, Fall on! God is our Strength!"

The governor's men answered:

"Hey for St. Marys!"

In the words of the Puritan chronicler, "The charge was fierce and sharp." The battle was soon over except for the resistance of a small company who "from behind a great fallen tree, galled us." The St. Marys men surrendered after a promise of quarter. The governor's force lost fifty men killed or wounded, including Stone himself wounded in the shoulder, and all but four or five captured. The Puritans admitted to losing two in the field and two later of wounds. Rummaging through the defeated camp, the Puritans found "heaps of rosary beads" and other "trash."

Despite their promise of quarter, the Roundheads convened a court-martial. Ten men, including Governor Stone, were condemned to death. Four were shot before the pleas of the wives of the others, seconded by some of the Puritan soldiery, stayed the executions. The prisoners of lower rank were released while their leaders, including the governor, were held until the Puritans decided what to do with them.

The Roundheads now had second thoughts about defiance of the governor and his authority from England. Stone they held incommunicado. His wife was to write bitterly that she was not allowed to tend her wounded husband. Finally they released him after extracting an oath of silence. Each side eventually went to press in England to vindicate itself. Pamphlets appeared under titles such as "Babylon's Fall" and "Babylon's Fall Refuted." Depositions were made and sworn; appeals were lodged with Cromwell and Baltimore; charges and countercharges flew. Cromwell was preoccupied with problems closer to England rather than remote colonial bickerings; Baltimore was more interested in reasserting his authority rather than in vengeance. In the end, the proprietor's control was restored and restitution made to those who suffered in the civil struggle. Among the compensated was the widow of one of those executed after the Battle of the Severn.

Oyster Tonging in the Chesapeake

V

Economic History of the Tidewater

VERRAZANO saw the mouth of the Chesapeake in 1524 and perhaps sailed up the Eastern Shore as far as the Pocomoke River. His is the first European record of the Bay. A Spanish friar, Brother Carrera, described a voyage to the Chesapeake in 1572. The pilots of the expedition who—he assures us—had sailed a great deal, said it possessed the largest and best ports in the world, many deepwater harbors, each better than the next. The Bay, which he said was named Mother of God, was three leagues at its mouth and thirty in depth; at the end of it began the other sea, the Pacific. Sixteen years later Captain Vincente Gonzales sailed to the end of the Chesapeake—probably the first European to see the upper Bay.

By the close of the 16th century England was ripe for overseas adventure. Hakluyt urged patriotic, enterprising Englishmen to bestir themselves and emulate the Spanish and Portuguese by planting colonies abroad. First, Renaissance types such as Raleigh and Gilbert made fruitless attempts to establish settlements in North America, or Virginia as the English called it. The challenge of settling a colony across three thousand miles of ocean exceeded the resources of any single individual. Where the lone adventurer failed, however, the joint stock company succeeded. As a business organized for trading and chartered by the Crown, the group was able to amass the necessary capital and support for a successful colony in the New World. Elizabeth chartered the Company of Gentlemen Adventurers of London who planted, supported and promoted the first permanent settlement. In the end they lost their investment, but not until Jamestown had been settled.

The Englishmen who sponsored the company knew little of the conditions the colonists would actually face, and their instructions reflected their ignorance. Jamestown's unfortunate location, it is said, was the result of such unwise guidance. After exploring the lower James for 11 days and rejecting many sites, the colonists finally selected Jamestown Island.

Following instructions to pick a spot easy to defend, they chose a malarial swamp where disease and discomfort plagued the settlement throughout its life.

The settlement grew so slowly that after ten years the population numbered only 350. These few worked hard, however, and by 1619 plantations lined both banks of the James as far as the Appomattox, extending four to six miles inland. Five years later plantations had been established as far upstream as the head of navigation, where Richmond now stands. By 1630 lands along the York, the next river to the north, were being cleared. Settlements continued to spread, first along the major rivers and then following the smaller tributaries into the many necks of land that form Tidewater Virginia. Settlement in Maryland began with the *Ark* and the *Dove* in 1634 and soon expanded to meet the Virginia colonists along the Potomac.

Several factors contributed to the rise of plantations along the Bay Foremost was the accessibility of the area to oceangoing shipping from England. Rivers and streams throughout Tidewater made transportation of people and goods relatively easy, inexpensive, and fast—two to three months for an Atlantic crossing. Land was available almost for the taking and proved to be fertile, especially for tobacco. The European market for the "sot weed" was expanding and profits from tobacco were high, so high that colonists were reluctant to grow other crops. Jamestown, for example, found it necessary to pass ordinances requiring colonists to plant fixed percentages of their land in corn, and forbidding tobacco growing in the streets. Tobacco soon became the principal export from the Bay area, and the plantation developed as the best way to produce it.

Eastern Shore

Efficient production required large tracts of land, generally 250 to 500 acres. The fields might be contiguous or might be scattered over a small area. Tobacco quickly exhausted the soil, and "new ground" had to be brought continually into cultivation. Cheap and plentiful labor was provided by slaves. Ralph H. Brown, in *Historical Geography of the United*

States, has described the growing and marketing process. When land had been cleared, the stumps were grubbed out and the trees burned or split for fence rails. In early spring tobacco seedbeds were started, sometimes under cloth, in protected spots in nearby woods. During April and May the hands "pitched" or transplanted the seedlings in hills three or four feet apart. Throughout the long growing season the plants were cultivated using hand tools—sprouting hoes, narrow hoes, and hilling hoes. The colonists rarely fertilized; the first recorded import of fertilizer reached Baltimore from Peru about 1840. Suckers were culled and insects picked by hand. Field hands harvested the plants, cutting them with knives and threading them on pointed sticks to be hung in closely spaced rows for barn curing. The cured leaves were picked from the stalk, pressed or "prized" into bundles, and packed in hogsheads weighing several hundred pounds. Boats or wagons carried the hogsheads to the riverside wharf. Sometimes the barrels were rolled along the road, but rolling damaged the leaves and lowered the price. Colonial law required that the leaves be inspected and tagged at a public warehouse. These tags circulated as a form of currency throughout Tidewater.

From the inspection procedure evolved the tobacco auction, a time-honored custom that has lasted to this day. Piles of tobacco cover the warehouse floor, where buyers examine them, inspecting and grading the leaf. Moving from bundle to bundle, the auctioneer leads the bidding in a loud singsong. Unintelligible to the outsider, his chant leads quickly to a sale. The price, grade, and buyer's name are tagged to the pile, and the auctioneer and buyers hurry to the next bundle of leaf. The auction proceeds at an astonishing rate, knocking down as many as 240 lots in an hour.

The plantation owner of the 18th century lived in some style, although even the richest were only moderately wealthy by contemporary English standards. His ships unloaded their tobacco at the London docks and took on board the luxuries of England and the continent—wines, fine furniture, glassware, china—together with manufactured goods unavailable in the New World. The wealthiest sometimes brought out master builders to design and supervise construction of their mansions. One lived sumptuously enough to be dubbed "King" Carter. Others were heavily in debt to merchants at home in England, and all were faced by the unpleasant prospect of falling tobacco prices. Leisure gave them time for politics, and Tidewater Maryland and Virginia produced many Colonial and Revolutionary statesmen.

Although the Crown and proprietors wanted towns and chartered hundreds of them, the plantation economy discouraged their growth. The plantation performed many urban functions: cobbling, clothesmaking, brick manufacture, repairs. Jamestown and St. Marys, originally colonial capitals, died as towns when the seat of government was removed else-

Sandy Point Light

where. Williamsburg, Yorktown, Lancaster, Cambridge, Chestertown, and many other Tidewater towns, have roots in colonial days but never developed in size or importance. The growth of the big cities of the Bay area awaited another phase of its economic history.

Boatyard on Mill Creek

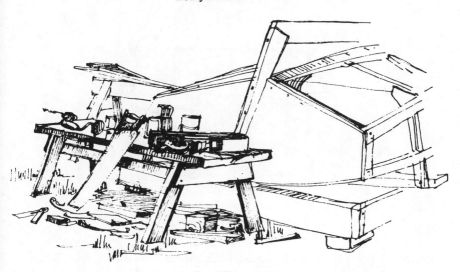

Boat Carpentry

Transportation interacting with topography played a major part in the development of Norfolk and Baltimore, the only large cities on the Bay. Moving inland by ship and boat from their first settlements, the colonists sooner or later found their way upriver barred by rapids. At the sites of Havre de Grace, Baltimore, Washington, Fredericksburg, Richmond, and

Petersburg they reached the head of navigation of the Susquehanna, Patapsco, Potomac, Rappahannock, James, and Appomattox Rivers. A contour connecting these cities follows the junction of the coastal plain with the Piedmont plateau and is known as the fall line, from the waterfalls or rapids located there. Here travelers stopped for food and lodging, and goods were unloaded from watercraft, stored, and reloaded for overland transport. As the flow of settlers moved west, towns sprang up all along the fall line.

Baltimore was founded in 1729 by colonial legislature, with 60 acres of land laid out in 60 lots. To insure its success as a port, the town was made a privileged place for landing, loading, and selling goods. Its excellent

Screw-pile Lighthouse

natural harbor gave it an additional advantage, and its location, 75 miles west of Philadelphia, gave good land access to the rich hinterland of southern Pennsylvania and the Maryland Piedmont. Rivers tumbling over the fall line powered waterwheels and mills. As an added incentive to development, the town held a fair every spring and fall during which the town police suspended arrests except for felony and breach of the peace.

The town prospered. A 1752 sketch shows 25 substantial looking, well separated houses on the fields and hills behind the harbor. Twenty years later Baltimore, with 17,000 inhabitants, was the largest town in the colony.

In 1787 it boasted 2,000 houses; in 1795, 3,000. A contemporary Creole writer, Moreau de St. Méry, claimed that:

> This rather large city, situated on an arm of the Patapsco River, is the county seat and the most extensive and flourishing commercial center in Maryland. It extends from Harris Creek in the south to the great branch of the Patapsco, and increases each day amazingly.

Baltimore shipowners operated over 200 ships, and the city's exports were valued at $5,300,000. In 1802 it had become the fourth largest port in the new Republic, and its industries included refineries, distilleries, tobacco factories, rope walks, paper mills, cotton mills, nail and shoe factories, tanneries, and lumber yards.

With its spacious harbor at Hampton Roads, Norfolk started as the *entrepot* for the southern end of the Chesapeake. There are no deep rivers between the James and Albemarle Sound 50 miles to the south. Hence cargoes to and from southeastern Virginia and northeastern North Carolina were loaded, offloaded, stored, and sometimes bought and sold in Norfolk.

Commerce with the plantations originally bypassed Norfolk, the ships working their way from the Virginia Capes up the Bay and rivers directly to the planters' wharves. Virginia ordinances attempted to regulate commerce and foster port development by requiring ships to load exports at Norfolk and other central points, but they were generally ignored. In the 18th century, however, oceangoing ships grew in size, and their deeper draft and reduced maneuverability made them harder to handle in inland rivers and streams. Direct trade with the plantations decreased, since the large ships came more frequently to Norfolk to offload their cargoes. There the goods were taken on board smaller craft whose shoal draft and local crews facilitated navigation in Tidewater or down the coast to Albemarle Sound for delivery to the ultimate consignee. On the return voyage to Norfolk, the Bay craft and coastal schooners carried tobacco, lumber, livestock, and naval stores—the colonists' next most valuable export. Virginia-owned vessels as well as English and New England craft transshipped the cargoes to Britain and the West Indies. The shipping business attracted merchants, artisans, shipowners, captains, and sailors, and the Hampton Roads ports prospered accordingly.

De St. Méry visited Norfolk in the 1790s and reported it as Virginia's foremost port. Eighty deepwater vessels, ten coasters, and 100 Bay craft operated from Norfolk. Norfolk-built ships, he wrote, were highly regarded for their speed, especially the brigs and schooners. Since the Revolution, direct commerce with England had almost vanished. Consumer goods came chiefly from Baltimore, New York, and Philadelphia, while considerable amounts of lumber, barrel staves, shingles, flour, corn, and cattle were shipped to the Antilles. On a critical note, he added that the piers and warehouses were poorly built and in disrepair, and the ship-worms were a menace from June to September.

As early as 1750, the plantation system showed signs of decay. Farmed-out tobacco fields reverted to sedge and scrub pine or were occasionally seeded to corn and wheat. Yields were poor and wheat fields seldom pro-duced more than ten bushels to the acre. Gradually the planters were forced to abandon their cash crop—tobacco—and shift to diversified sub-sistence farming. With the change came a loss of income, lower standards of living, and decreased population. In the century and a quarter after the first census of 1790, seven Tidewater counties lost population despite the 25-fold increase nationwide.

Bay Freighter at Cambridge

De St. Méry found the western shore along the Patuxent a "wretched place" with "miserable buildings." In 1794, he reported, the crops were rye, oats, and tobacco, with some effort to grow cotton. Andrew Weld, a British traveler of the same period, thought the countryside equally un-attractive. The Potomac ferryhouse at Port Tobacco was "one of those old, dilapidated mansions that formerly was the residence, perhaps, of some wealthy planter . . . now the picture of wretchedness and poverty." He described "the remains of several good houses which show that the country was once very different from what it is now . . . perfect wilderness . . . for miles altogether." The English writer, Frances Trollope, left

Baltimore Dock

an unflattering description of the countryside between Washington and Richmond in the 1830s—abandoned, eroded fields traversed by bad roads.

Records of Providence Forge plantation on the Chicahominy between Richmond and Norfolk reflect the changes. In the 1820s the estate owned 3,000 acres and 110 slaves. Tobacco occupied only three or four acres;

corn, broomcorn, wheat (1,500 bushels in 1830), vegetables, and a small amount of cotton were the main crops. Providence Forge owned 15 mules and horses, 90 cattle, 500 sheep, and 200 hogs. From the Chicahominy came shad and herring and in winter, ice to be cut and stored. It was a struggle for the plantation to support slaves, managers, owners, and families. Like many others, Providence Forge had become "slave-poor" with too many mouths to feed. Some Tidewater planters began to export their slaves to the lower Mississippi valley where cotton, another crop demanding much labor, was beginning its reign. Thus the decline of the Bay tobacco plantation contributed to the westward spread of slavery with its cataclysmic effects on the economics, politics and history of the south.

In the first half of the 19th century, Tidewater fell behind the expanding north and west both in economic strength and political influence. Virginia, for example, had furnished seven of the country's first 12 presidents but was not to produce another until Woodrow Wilson took office in 1913. To regain their former positions, Marylanders and Virginians sought to capture the trade from the west. Baltimore and Norfolk struggled to compete with the fall line towns, with northern ports, and with each other. George Washington had hoped that the Potomac would become a great industrial valley, the avenue of commerce linking the east and the nation's capital with the Ohio Valley. He planned a canal along the Virginia shore upriver from Georgetown, and formed the Potowmack Company to build it. With his death in 1799 the canal halted. The Erie Canal, completed in 1825, brought a boom to New York City, now the outlet for the entire Great Lakes. Fearing that New York would dominate

Naval Refrigerator Ship

the western trade, one group of southern businessmen pushed for a canal up the Potomac and over the mountains to Ohio and a rival Baltimore company promoted a railway from Baltimore to Pittsburg. Both projects began on Independence Day, 1828, when President Adams broke ground for the canal at Little Falls and Charles Carroll of Carrollton—the last surviving signer of the Declaration of Independence—broke ground for the railroad in Baltimore. Later Virginia, urged by Richmond and Petersburg, built a canal system between Richmond and the west. Norfolk replied with a request for state aid in developing railroads to the Roanoke River and to Petersburg, canals to Albemarle Sound, and steam navigation on the Chesapeake. The first steam vessel connecting Norfolk and Baltimore went into service in 1817, and the Old Bay Line, famous in the annals of steamboat navigation on the Chesapeake, went into business in the 1840s. In 1829 the Chesapeake and Delaware Canal, first envisioned in 1679, opened and connected the upper Bay with the Delaware River at Reedy Point.

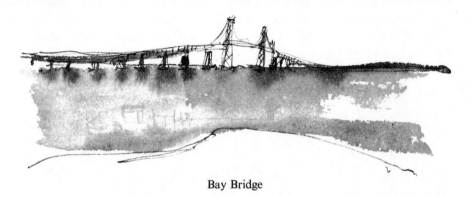

Bay Bridge

Fate favored Baltimore and Maryland over Norfolk and Virginia. Railroads proved more efficient and profitable than canals, and the "B and O" not only drained the products of Ohio into Baltimore but also diverted much of the trade from northern and western Virginia. Today Baltimore is a bigger port and a bigger city. Although as a manufacturing center Baltimore will probably keep her lead, developments in the shipping industry may give Norfolk and the Hampton Roads area an advantage as a port. The drafts of "supertankers" and "supercarriers" require deep channels, and Baltimore is 150 miles up the Bay from Hampton Roads. Baltimore is now served by a 42-foot channel, while the shorter channel from the Virginia Capes is being deepened to 45 feet. The bridge tunnel from Cape Charles to Little Creek would permit channel depths of 60 feet. Dredging is expensive, and its shorter distance from the ocean favors Hampton Roads over Baltimore if a deeper channel is to be created.

Another innovation, the container ship, has pitted the two ports against each other. The container ship loads cargo by the boxful. Loose packages and other items of freight are consolidated in standard size boxes especially designed for handling as a unit on ship, truck, or rail car. The system reduces pilferage and, through specialized but costly handling equipment, speeds shipping by as much as 100%. Container ships have revolutionized the industry, placing a premium on speed and efficiency in handling cargo. The North Atlantic container route appears able to support only two terminals on the U.S. east coast. New York has naturally become the leading port, but Baltimore and Hampton Roads are fighting for second place. Baltimore has the advantages of routes in two directions —south by the Bay and north by the Chesapeake and Delaware Canal— and of better existing facilities. Norfolk and the Hampton Roads ports, however, have a 300-mile, 20-hour advantage because of their proximity to the Capes. In the opinion of shipping expert W. Gregory Halpin, Baltimore has a slight edge with an excellent chance of staying ahead if the Chesapeake and Delaware Canal is deepened. The competition between the ports, now in its third century, will be keen and the outcome is difficult to predict.

Tobacco Barn

Although the high profits and style of life of the plantation system have vanished, agriculture remains important in the Bay area. Tidewater has particular advantages for truck farming; level topography, sandy soil, equable climate, abundant sun and rain. Sandy soils and heavy rainfall absorb the warmth and hold the moisture needed for watery products. Cheap labor, an advanced season, nearby urban markets, and ready means for shipping the perishable products are all available. In 1854 the steamer

Roanoke loaded the first shipment of 200 barrels of garden truck from the Eastern Shore for New York. Chesapeake Bay craft carried produce from the landings and docks of the Eastern Shore to Baltimore, which became one of the largest canning cities. At first ice was shipped from Maine for preserving the produce, but artificial ice plants, appearing first in Norfolk

Ore Carriers Waiting to Unload at Baltimore

in 1892, proved more economical. In 1887 the railroads, long delayed by the ease and economy of freighting by water, reached the Eastern Shore. Faster marketing by train and later by truck, the use of ice and refrigerator cars, and the growth of the canning and freezing industries opened new opportunities for agriculture. Larger urban populations and changing consumer tastes have also expanded the market for fresh foods.

In 1900 farmers on the Eastern Shore of Virginia planted 20,000 acres in their principal money crop, Irish and sweet potatoes. A crop of corn could usually follow the Irish potatoes before the first frost ended the long growing season. Kale, cabbage, onions, strawberries, and tomatoes were also grown. Twenty years later, over 50,000 acres were in potatoes. By 1960 the pattern had changed somewhat, with soybeans, potatoes, and tomatoes as the main crops and poultry as another major product.

Truck farming is a risky business. Produce is extremely perishable, and fluctuating market values make timing particularly important. Weather is critical. Frost, freezes, droughts, or excessive rain can destroy a crop and require costly replanting several times in a growing season. At the time of marketing, grade, color, and size have a great effect on prices. To reduce his risk, the farmer can contract in advance with the cannery for delivery at a fixed price. He can also choose between the truck market which is highly sensitive to timing, and the canners, who require a steady supply. New means of preservation by canning and quick freezing further decrease the emphasis on timing, but the risks remain. In a good year the truck farmer makes high profits; a poor season may break him.

Manufacturing has become important, particularly in the upper Bay and in industries requiring cheap transportation by water for raw materials or finished product. The Bethlehem Steel plant at Sparrows Point is the largest in the world, fed by a long line of ore carriers standing up the Bay. Chemicals, cement, and oil are important industries. Shipbuilding and repair go on at Baltimore, Newport News, and Portsmouth, and fishing and seafood processing retain their long-standing place in the economics of the Bay area.

Crowding the Bay country on the north and west is "megalopolis," a new type of region where the distinction between city and country disappears as urban centers grow together to form one continuous suburb. Megalopolis stretches from Boston to Washington and, according to other geographers, to Richmond or Norfolk. In this economic hinge of the country, agriculture has become revolutionized, woodland and wildlife threatened, and land usage drastically modified. Manufacturing and commercial organization is changing simultaneously. Megalopolis seems destined to become the wealthiest, most densely populated, and most productive urban area in the world. In the Bay country, though, traditional

Oyster Tonger

ways survive. Oysters, clams, and crabs continue to provide work for a diminishing but tenacious band of watermen. Tobacco, the traditional Tidewater crop, is raised, cured in tobacco barns, and sold at auctions where the chant of the auctioneer still sounds. Boatyards thrive, although their craftsmen work increasingly with fiberglass and less with pine and oak. The past dies slowly; the charm of the Chesapeake lies in its blend of the old with the new.

VI

Bay Country Forests

FOR MANY YEARS naturalists tended to study each class of living organisms separately from all others. Ornithologists specialized in birds; mammalogists in quadrupeds; botanists in plants; ichthyologists in fish; entomologists in insects. Climatologists and earth scientists, for their part, concentrated on their fields and ignored the living world. It is only in the past fifty years that scientists have recognized the importance of the relationships among living things and the conditions under which they live. This realization gave birth to the discipline called ecology: the study of organisms, their environment, and all the interrelationships between the two. Ecologists are concerned, for example, with the effect of lumbering on forest soil; the best breed of livestock for a given range, the effect of pesticides on birds of prey; the "carbon cycle"—the flow of carbon compounds from living to nonliving back to living matter. Their studies concern the ecosystem—the interacting unit comprising the community of living things and the habitat in which they dwell.

Ecologists have evolved the concept of the "web of life"—the complex set of pathways by which matter and energy flow among organisms. A single pathway is called a food chain. Grass, for example, is eaten by a grasshopper which is eaten by a lizard which is eaten by a hawk which eventually, through decomposers, returns to the soil to give nutrients to the grass. At the bottom of every chain is a plant, for only green plants can, through direct use of solar energy, transform inorganic, inedible matter— carbon dioxide, water, minerals—into sugars and other edible hydrocarbon compounds.

Plants influence other organisms not only by supplying food. They provide shelter—meadows for insects and small mammals, marshes for muskrats and blackbirds, treetops for squirrels and warblers, hollow trees for raccoons and bears. Even more important, they continue to regenerate the atmosphere's oxygen supply. In photosynthesis, green plants take in water from the soil, carbon dioxide from the air, and energy from sunlight. The process yields not only food in the form of hydrocarbons but another necessity—oxygen. The reaction takes place within tiny cells called chloroplasts. These contain the substance chlorophyll which gives green plants their color and also catalyzes the complex chemical reaction of photosynthesis. The hydrocarbons—complicated molecules of carbon, hydrogen, and oxygen—go into the plants' flowers, fruit, seeds, branches, trunks, and roots; the oxygen passes into the atmosphere through tiny openings in the leaves called stomatas.

In any ecosystem, then, vegetation is the dominant element, linking the environment with the organism. Plants respond more directly to their physical environment—temperature, rainfall, soil—than do other organisms, and they are at the base of the food chains of all living things. Ecologists therefore divide the world into parts according to their respective native plant life. In North America the pioneer ecologist was Dr. C. Hart Merriam, first chief of the U.S. Biological Survey. In 1892 he published the first of a series of papers on what he termed "life zones." Merriam saw temperature as the most important factor of the environment. Continuing his efforts to understand why organisms are distributed as they are, he found that he had overemphasized the influence of temperature and underemphasized that of rainfall. He finally settled on a division of the continent into three regions—Boreal, Austral, and Tropical. These he subdivided into zones and the zones into humid and dry divisions. Each zone is characterized by a particular type of vegetation: coniferous forests in the Canadian zone, pines in the humid division of the Lower Austral. The vegetation, in turn, to a large extent determines the resident species of animals and birds.

Other naturalists have divided North America in different ways. Professor Lee R. Dice of the University of Michigan identifies 28 "biotic provinces"; ornithologist Frank A. Pitelka counts seven "biomes"; ecologist Jack McCormick of the Philadelphia Academy of Natural Sciences defines seven "forest regions" while his fellow ecologist Ivan T. Sanderson plots 11 "belts" of vegetation which he further subdivides into 21 "natural provinces"; Professor Victor E. Shelford of the University of Illinois conceives of 12 "major natural communities." The problem is, on the one hand, to establish areas small enough to be homogeneous without, on the other hand, proliferating them until they become too numerous to provide useful generalizations.

In any case, the Chesapeake lies near the junction of three zones. According to Sanderson, the Bay is in the center of the Northeast Coastal Fringe Province, sandwiched between Appalachia and the Southern Pine Belt. His Appalachia extends west from the fall line and his Southern Pine Belt south below Pamlico Sound and the Tar River. Merriam places the bulk of the Bay in the Humid Division of the Upper Austral Zone, more briefly termed the Carolinian. The extreme southeastern corner of the Bay, from Cape Henry to Hampton Roads, lies in the Humid Division of the Lower Austral Zone, also called Austroriparian or Louisianan. Just above the headwaters of the Bay is the Transition or Alleghanian, whose border stretches from Long Island across northern New Jersey and northeastern Pennsylvania to the Alleghany Mountains.

Oak-Hickory Forest

From the point of view of vegetation, as described by Braun, Shelford, and others, the Bay spans three forest regions. At the extreme north is the oak-chestnut region, in the center the oak-hickory, and at the southern end the ecotone or transition zone between oak-hickory and maritime.

The ecotone consists largely of pinelands. The boundaries are not sharp, and the regions blend to some extent.

Throughout the Alleghanian, Carolinian, and Louisianan life zones the climax vegetation is a deciduous forest. By climax, ecologists mean the final, equilibrium condition which the living community attains. After a

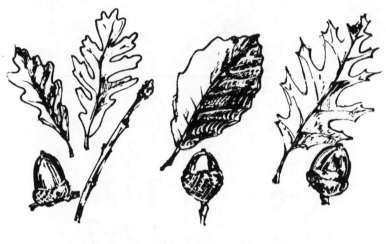

White Oak   Swamp White Oak   Black Oak

forest fire, for example, vegetation passes through a succession of stages, termed a sere, before it regains its original condition. It was a climax oak-hickory forest that confronted the seventeenth century settlers at Jamestown; the same vegetation bordered the entire Chesapeake except at the extreme north and extreme south.

In a climax oak-hickory woods the trees reach 75 feet in height with trunks two feet in diameter. A few sweet gum, tulip poplar and—before they were destroyed by a nationwide blight—chestnuts grew among the more numerous hickories. The treetops, nearly continuous, shade about 90 percent of the forest floor. Below the treetops the crowns form a layer some 50 feet deep with its lower boundary 30 to 40 feet above the forest floor. This region of leaves, twigs, and branches forms a biotic community itself, the canopy layer. Here is the habitat of the flying squirrels, of the warblers, and of the insects—sometimes more than a thousand of the latter for every square yard of the canopy's surface. Here grow the acorns and hickory nuts so important as a food for forest birds and animals. A large white oak may produce 15,000 acorns in a season; the mast crop of a forest of nut trees controls to a large extent the size of its population of squirrel, deer, and bear.

Below the canopy is another community, the understory tree layer. Here are younger oaks, hickories, and other canopy varieties as well as shorter species. Near the Bay one finds dogwood, holly, and red maple in the understory. These make do with a fraction of the sun's rays that penetrate the canopy; short trees survive in a climax forest only if they thrive in the shade or if a break in the canopy lets sunlight in. The understory shelters its own population of organisms—caterpillars, snails, wood thrushes, Acadian flycatchers. As the air temperature rises in early spring, before the leaves of the canopy have opened, the understory trees enjoy their day in the sun. Now they receive their greatest share of sunlight; dogwood and Judas trees burst into bloom and the woods are at their loveliest.

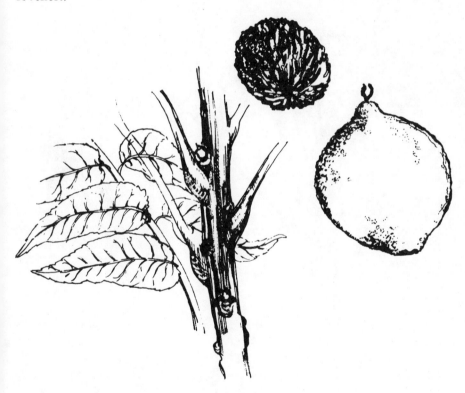

Black Walnut

The shrub layer forms a third forest community comprising tree seedlings and high shrubs—laurel, poison ivy, sumac. These receive even less light than the understory, which has added its shade to that of the canopy. Like it, the shrub layer is most dense at the edges of natural and man-made clearings. Mammal and bird life is plentiful in this community. Many birds build their nests at that height, and more feed there. Deer browse on shrubs and seedlings; a heavy deer population strongly affects the development and ultimate makeup of a wooded area. Shelford emphasizes that the deciduous forest is not exclusively plant controlled: "The plants control certain conditions, but the animals control the plants of the next generation . . . The forest stands are what the deer and associated animals permit to grow from what they miss in their feeding." The present

Tuliptree   Tuliptree Seed Cone

abundance of deer around the Bay is a result of the change from deep woods to shrubs as a successive stage in abandoned fields and pastures of cutover woodland.

On the forest floor is the herb layer, defined as the region from the ground up to a height of one meter. Here grow ferns, mosses, skunk cabbage, crowsfoot, and other plants requiring a minimum of sunlight. Wildflowers of the herb layer concentrate their photosynthetic activity in earliest spring, before canopy or understory trees are in leaf. Increasing solar radiation causes these herbs to put out leaves and blossom quickly. By the time the canopy's shade closes over the forest floor, they have made the season's food, stored it in roots or underground stems, and seeded themselves. Many varieties then disappear, their above-ground parts dead, to await the next spring and repeat the cycle.

In the herb layer live beetles, millipedes, snakes, shrews, mice, ovenbirds, and towhees. On the forest floor and just below it live the decomposers, the microorganisms of the soil that change the proteins of fallen leaves and animal bodies back into the compounds that feed plants. Hence the soil is both the beginning and the end of the forest's web of life.

Shelford has given an avowedly crude description of the biota of a typical ten square miles of a climax Carolinian forest. It includes three quarters of a million trees of over 3 inches diameter breast high (a standard measurement in forestry, abbreviated d.b.h.) and slightly more under 3 inches d.b.h. The plot contains almost three million shrubs and several hundred million herbs. For each tree, then, there are about 1.1 seedlings, 4 shrubs, and 500 plants. In the ten square miles, the summer invertebrate population reaches more than 25 billion, mainly spiders and insects. The bird population averages 20 to 50 hawks and owls, several hundred turkeys, and perhaps 7500 pairs of smaller birds, about one per hundred trees. Small mammals in the tract average several hundred thousand mice and several tens of thousands of squirrels. Without the interference of man, ten square miles would also contain two or three wolves and cougars, half a dozen bears, several dozen foxes and wildcats, and several hundred whitetail deer and elk.

There is little or no truly climax forest in the Bay country today; four or five centuries are required before a forest reaches its final equilibrium stage. A few trees of that age remain: the Wye oak on Maryland's Eastern Shore is estimated to be over 400 years old. It is one of the largest white oaks in the United States—95 feet high, 165 feet in horizontal spread, and 21 feet around the trunk. In Annapolis the Treaty Tree still grows on the grounds of St. Johns College—a tulip poplar 29 feet in circumference, it is believed to be over 600 years old. In 1652, already mature, its branches shaded colonial officials and chiefs of the Susquehanna Indians as they signed the treaty that was to give the tree its name. A forest of oaks and poplars like these would be impressive indeed. Hopefully in a century or two the state forests of the Chesapeake will reach the climax of their sere. In the meantime, one can see examples of all the intermediate stages.

During its first few years an abandoned pasture or field grows over with grasses and weeds—ragweed, goldweed, Queen Anne's lace. Many small farmers are shifting to other occupations, and this habitat occurs more and more frequently. An equally common sight in the Bay area is a stand of sumac, bayberry, greenbrier, pokeweed, and a few pine and cedar seedlings. These cover a field that has been abandoned from five to ten years. Small game is usually plentiful—cottontail and bobwhite—as well as meadowlarks, harvest mice, and goldfinches. Nearby one often sees a stand of scrub pine a dozen feet high. It has been growing ten years or

Beech Trees

more. Its solid canopy shades out the undergrowth; in another fifteen years the ground will be a soft bed of needles, easy to walk on and a pleasant site for a camp. With the undergrowth go the cottontail and bobwhite, replaced by a new group of birds and animals—squirrels, possum, bluejays, titmice, and pine warblers.

A mixed evergreen-deciduous woods is the next stage. Pine and cedar seedlings that sprouted in the sun of the old field cannot survive in the

deep shade of the pine woods. The evergreens do not reproduce themselves, but seeds of the deciduous trees, carried by wind, animals, or birds,
gradually reach the humus of the forest floor. Adapted to growth in the
shade, they take root and thrive beneath the pine boughs. Gradually they
grow taller and, in 30 to 40 years, break through the pine canopy into the
sun. The mixed pine and deciduous woods, if untouched by man, is in-
evitably on its way to the climax oak-hickory stage. The tall hardwoods,
as they reach the sun, spread their branches over the pines and cut off their
supply of solar energy. The evergreens die, and the second growth deciduous forest remains until fire or cutting repeats the cycle.

In a wood developed from a field or pasture or from a clean cut forest,
the mature climax trees are of nearly the same age and size. They form a
widespread, uniform canopy with few breaks. As a consequence the shrub
and herb layers are sparse and the understory includes only deciduous

Black Walnut

species. Such a community harbors few animals and birds as compared to
the earlier stages, where the dense, sunlit shrubs and seedlings provided
ample food and shelter. In a hundred-year-old second growth oak-hickory
stand, one sees and hears woodpeckers, tanagers, vireos, and ovenbirds,
but few other species. The most conspicuous animals are the gray squirrels. In a fully mature climax forest, on the other hand, trees are of many
different ages. The oldest, scattered throughout the stand, die or fall in
windstorms, breaking the canopy and passing sunlight to the lower layers.
Herbs and shrubs multiply in the new clearing, and pine and cedar spring
up among the hardwoods. The added cover and food bring with them
different and more numerous organisms. Understory deciduous trees,
reaching for the sun, grow rapidly to fill in the gap in the canopy. As one
opening fills, however, another ancient tree topples and a new clearing

appears. With clearings scattered throughout the stand, mature forests support far more wildlife than new second growth woods.

There is a similar change when man clears a road or power line right-of-way through a second growth forest. Here the sun penetrates the canopy, and the understory, herb, and shrub layers develop rapidly. All along the new edge wildlife increases in response to the increase in food and cover. Wildlife managers take advantage of this technique by clearing small plots throughout the forests and planting them with lespedeza, multiflora rose, milo, and other food-bearing plants. Even a few "wildlife clearings" in a solid forest are enough to keep the game population high.

Loblolly Pines

The Piedmont Plateau borders the extreme north shore of the Bay between the Elk River and the Susquehanna. Higher and more rolling than the coastal plain to the south, this terrain supports a different climax vegetation, an oak-chestnut forest. There are no mature chestnut trees, however, because of the chestnut blight. This disease came to the United States about 1900 with the planting of Chinese chestnut trees in New York. It spread north and south throughout the chestnuts of the Appalachians and the Piedmont Plateau. By 1940 the old trees were dead. Sprouts continue to grow from the roots of the dead trees, but they too become diseased, wither, and die. What used to be an oak-chestnut forest is now maturing as a mixture of oaks—red oak, white oak, chestnut oak—and tulip poplar.

Farther south, in Calvert County near the Patuxent, an isolated stand of American chestnut has somehow resisted the blight, together with a blight-resistant hybrid of American and Chinese chestnuts. These give hope that the chestnut may some day regain its former range.

Just as the oak-chestnut forest touches the Bay's northern tip, the pine-land ecotone borders its southern end. All biomes merge gradually into their neighbors, but sometimes the transitional zone is large enough to merit a designation of its own. This is the case in the southern piney woods. These merge on the west with the oak-hickory climax, characteristic not only of the Chesapeake but of most of the Coastal Plain, and on the east with various types of coastal vegetation. The pine woods were originally—

Loblolly Pines on Lower Potomac

before the white man—a result of forest fires. Set either by Indians to drive game or naturally by lightning, fires destroyed deciduous trees, both mature and seedlings. Pine saplings, especially those of longleaf pine, resist fire damage, and these survived. The post-fire stage, then, became a pine forest, termed a "fire subclimax." As in the adjacent regions, decidu-ous trees tend to succeed the pines. Over the last three centuries, however, this ecotone has been particularly influenced by man-made fires and by man's clean cutting. The deciduous climax forest has not been allowed to take its normal turn in the sere. As a consequence the piney woods are characteristic of a wide belt from the Bay south almost to the Gulf of Mexico.

The canopy of a Bay pine forest, some 75 to 100 feet above the ground, consists of loblolly or old-field pine mingled with occasional longleaf and shortleaf pines. The trees may be as much as 200 years old and three feet in diameter. The understory includes dogwood, holly, and other deciduous seedlings, although few pine stands are left uncut long enough for an understory to develop. The shrub layer includes smilax and honeysuckle; the herb layer is of wire grass, broom sedge, and crowsfoot. Deer, bear, turkey, and small mammals and birds are plentiful in very young or very old pine woods. In intermediate stages, where the floor is covered with pinestraw and there are few shrubs and bushes, game is nearly absent.

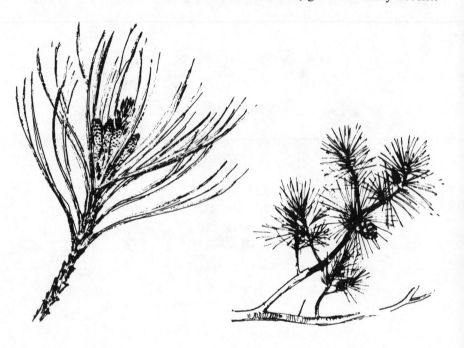

Loblolly Needles   Loblolly Branches

Throughout the Bay country, pine forests are on the increase. Faster growing than hardwoods, pines are a more profitable source of timber. A pine woods can be cut at an age of about 40 years; oak takes twice as long. Individuals and corporations, assisted by state authorities, are creating thousands of acres of pinelands, some from abandoned agricultural land and some from cutover deciduous forests. In 1966-67, for example, Virginians planted 55 million pine seedlings covering about 85,000 acres. Additional land reseeded naturally brought the total to over 100,000, much of it in the Tidewater. Such an extensive change from fields and deciduous forests to young pine woods has a pronounced ecological effect, principally through the change in food supply and cover.

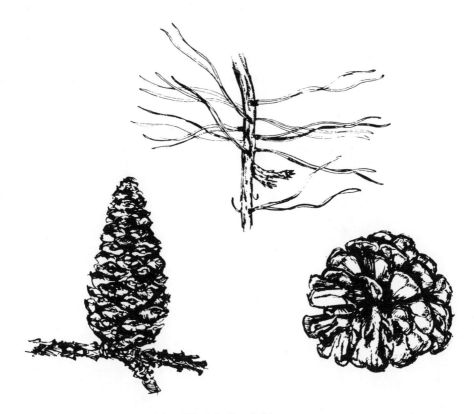

Virginia Scrub Pine

After the underbrush of the first five years has been shaded out, wildlife populations decline sharply because of the lack of food and cover. Fortunately game managers have developed management techniques which maintain strong wildlife populations at little expense to the timber owner. One technique is the maintenance of clearings, some planted to perennials and others mowed periodically to encourage natural vegetation. Leaving occasional islands or alternatively a scattering of single oak, hickory, and beech trees throughout the pine stand produces mast—an important wildlife food. Homes for animals and birds are provided by selecting and leaving at least two dozen trees per acre. Additional food and cover come from cutting back trees for 30 to 40 feet along access roads and utility right of

Western Maryland Forest

VII

Birds

TO THE GUNNER, the Chesapeake suggests geese in a grainfield or canvasbacks circling a duck blind. The fisherman pictures terns diving on a school of baitfish; the beach camper remembers gulls and sandpipers on the seashore. To the farmer, Bay birds can be meadowlarks whistling in a pasture or crows cawing in the corn. The bird watcher recalls "century runs"—lists of 100 or more species in a day's observation.

Two factors contribute to the variety of the Bay's birdlife: its range of environment and its location on a migration route. The environments are unusually varied because the Chesapeake spans nearly three life zones, each embracing a number of different habitats. At its southern extremity the Bay lies in the Austroriparian life zone; the bulk falls in the Carolinian; and the Alleghanian lies a hundred miles to the north and west up the Susquehanna. From the fall line at Havre de Grace through the coastal plain to the ocean at the Virginia Capes, the Bay washes a variety of habitats. Each habitat in each life zone attracts its own breeding population. In the winter the Atlantic flyways, converging at the Chesapeake, add flocks of waterfowl and other migratory species to the Bay's birdlife.

The characteristic breeding birds of the Austroriparian zone are those of the piney woods and warm waters; chuck-will's-widow, brown-headed nuthatch, Louisiana heron. Only the extreme southeastern corner of the Bay lies in this zone—the 20 miles of shoreline from Hampton Roads to Cape Henry together with the low country to the south. To the north, up the Bay, lies the Carolinian life zone. Its oak-pine subclimax attracts the fish crow, the tufted titmouse, and the hooded warbler. A third zone, the Alleghanian, reaches within 120 miles of the Bay where its lower boundary stretches from Long Island across northern New Jersey and northeastern Pennsylvania to the Alleghany mountains, Characteristically covered by a climax deciduous forest, this zone is the natural breeding habitat of the kingbird, the wood thrush, and the towhee.

53

Turkey Buzzard

Little Blue Heron   Great Blue Heron

along the Bay: from Cape Henry to Willoughby Spit, along the lower Potomac, at Sandy Point near Annapolis, at Elk Neck on the Eastern Shore. Shorter stretches of beach are numerous on both shores. Terns breed on only a few isolated beaches, but every stretch of sand attracts plovers and sandpipers. Mudflats and shallows extend into the Bay along most of its gently sloping shoreline; these are the hunting grounds of the

Canvasback

waders—herons, egrets, and bitterns. Together with the deeper waters they furnish food for the fish hawks, gulls, terns, cormorants, and skimmers. In the upper Bay the rivers are smaller and the water fresher. From a day sailer in the Severn or the Tred Avon one may see kingfishers and green herons at the water's edge, bluejays and woodpeckers on the wooded banks. A mile's paddle from a creek mouth to its head in a marsh can give the bird watcher a long list of water, shore, and woodland species. Even in urban areas, the water attracts birds in quantity and in variety. From a city lawn on the Lafayette River in Norfolk a casual count listed 31 species ranging from black skimmer to chimney swift.

the Arctic Ocean: Great Bear, Great Slave, Athabaska, Winnipeg, Huron, and Erie. The sloping sides converge at Delaware and Chesapeake Bays. The flyway continues southward as a narrow track along the Atlantic Coast to the Caribbean.

Scaup

Black Duck

Canada Geese

Old Squaw

Loon

Old Squaw

Down this funnel every autumn pour the waterfowl of almost half of Canada. In colonial days the flocks seemed numberless. An early traveller wrote in his journal:

> I must not forget to mention the great number of wild geese we saw here on the river. They rose not in flocks of ten, or twelve, or twenty or thirty, but continuously, wherever we pushed our way; and, as they made room for us, there was such an incessant clattering made with their wings upon the water when they rose, and such a noise of flying higher up, that it was all the time as if we were surrounded by a whirlwind or a storm. This proceeded not only from geese, but from ducks and other water-fowl; and it is not peculiar to this place alone, but it occurred on all the creeks and rivers we crossed, though they were most numerous in the morning and evening, when they are most easily shot.

As late as a hundred years ago Bay waterfowl were abundant. Gunning for the market was a livelihood for watermen; the housewife in Washington or Baltimore could buy canvasbacks or mallards as easily as chicken. Market hunters shot from sink boxes surrounded by hundreds of decoys.

Whistling Swan

Their guns were large, their seasons unlimited, and there were no bag limits. In the Chesapeake Bay Maritime Museum at St. Michaels is a 4-gauge shotgun reputed to have killed 700 ducks in a day. Commercial and sporting hunting pressure, together with the destruction of breeding grounds as civilization covered the continent, was too much for the waterfowl. Each fall brought fewer and smaller flocks to the Bay, and each spring fewer survivors flew north to breed. Geese and ducks were scarce; swans almost disappeared. In 1917 an ornithologist wrote unhappily:

> There is no safety for a swan in this country except it be high in the air or far out in open water . . . The great flocks that once frequented the coast in winter from Massachusetts to South Carolina are gone . . .

Today the swans are back, and the ducks and geese too. Half a century of conservation in the United States and Canada has made the change: research and legislation by the government, funds and restraint from shooters, interest and action on the part of nature lovers. The Migratory Bird Treaties of 1916 and 1937, between the United States, Canada, and Mexico, bound the governments to establish bag limits and hunting seasons and to stop summer shooting. Funds from hunting licenses,

mate was down to about 20 pairs. Throughout other parts of the Eastern United States their numbers are in similar decline. Their decrease may be a result of the increased use of insecticides. Scientists suspect that DDT, found in the embryos of unhatched eggs, may prevent them from hatching.

Whatever the reason, the eagle has become a rare sight and the Bay is poorer for it. Bald Eagle Point, near the mouth of the Choptank, remains

American Eagle

as a memorial. Ospreys are plentiful near the Point, and so are turkey buzzards. From a distance both of these large species resemble eagles; they can be distinguished by the cant of their wings. Ospreys soar with a bend in their wings; buzzards with their wings slanted upward in a shallow vee. The eagle keeps his wings flat. A bird watcher at Bald Eagle Point can see many birds of prey. The glasses show ospreys with their crooked wings and buzzards with vees, but no flat-winged eagle. He leaves disappointed but hopeful that the bald eagle may yet make his comeback like the waterfowl.

VIII

Mammals

WHEN THE FIRST Europeans entered Chesapeake Bay they found a climax biome—a community whose flora, fauna, and human inhabitants shared a stable interrelationship. The last major factors for change in the environment had been the recession of the glaciers at the close of the Pleistocene epoch and the migration of humans across the land bridge from Asia some 25,000 years earlier. An equilibrium had developed between the producers and the consumers, and food chains remained about the same, century after century. An ecologist, had such a scientist existed and studied the Bay country, would have found the woods and waters much the same at the birth of Christ as at the birth of Lord Baltimore.

He would have seen a nearly unbroken stand of oak and hickory along the upper and middle Bay with a transition to pine woods at the extreme lower end. Marshes lined extensive portions of the shoreline, particularly on the Eastern Shore. Indians lived on both shores, their average population density estimated by Professor V. E. Shelford of the University of Illinois as one to two per square mile. They shared the country with a variety of large mammals: whitetail deer, wolf, cougar, bobcat, black bear, elk and at the southern end an occasional manatee. Smaller mammals included gray and red fox, opossum, raccoon, gray, red and fox squirrels, muskrat, mink, otter, skunk and bats. To John Smith, in 1608, it was a region of "pleasant plaine hills and fertile valleys, one prettily crossing another . . . all overgrowne with trees and weedes being a plain wilderness as God first made it."

George Alsop, who came to the upper Bay as an indentured servant 50 years after Smith, listed eleven species of mammals: "The Elke, the Cat of the Mountain, the Rackoon, the Fox, the Beaver, the Otter, the Possum, the Hare, the Squirril, the Monack (chipmunk), the Musk-Rat, and several others whom I'le omit for brevity's sake inhabit here in Maryland in several droves and troops, ranging the woods at their pleasure."

Thompson Seton, famed Canadian naturalist, writer, and artist, cites records of New England deer caught in the ocean as far as five miles off-shore. The hairs of their winter coat contain air cells, which help the deer keep afloat in its long-distance swims.

The English colonists found two larger species of deer along the eastern seaboard. One, twice the size of the whitetail, with long pointed antlers, ranged both north and south of the Bay. The Indians called it *wapiti*. The other, still larger, with massive flattened antlers, inhabited northern New England and Nova Scotia. The Indians called it *mongsoa*. Neither animal

Whitetail Deer

had a counterpart in Britain. The nearest relative of the *wapiti* inhabited the Altai and Tashkent of central Asia; the closest relative of the *mongsoa* was the European elk of Scandinavia. As luck would have it, the English settlers misnamed the *wapiti* by calling it elk. The *mongsoa*, which properly should have been called elk, became moose.

Better field observers than taxonomists, the early colonists misnamed a number of other animals and birds. The English robin is no larger than a chickadee, but the homesick settlers gave that name to the first red-breasted bird they saw, changing a thrush into the American robin. In England the buzzard is a dark brown buteonine hawk; the colonists gave that name to an American vulture, similar in size and flight but different in color and shape. The American bison they misnamed buffalo; the skunk became a polecat. In natural history as in other ways, George Bernard Shaw observed accurately that America and England are *divided* by a common language.

In any case the colonists found the *wapiti* plentiful from the Bay westward. In 1666 George Alsop wrote of the Susquehanna Indians' winter hunts: "About November the best hunters draw off to several remote places of the woods where they know the Deer, Bear, and Elk useth . . ." The elk gave their name to Elk Neck, Elk River, Big Elk Creek, Elkton and Elk Mills at the head of the Bay and to Elk Ridge near the Patapsco. Hunting and clearing soon forced them first out of the coastal plain and then from the Piedmont. The last elk was killed in Virginia in 1844 in the Appalachians; the last recorded elk east of the Mississippi was shot in Pennsylvania in 1867.

In 1917 and again in 1936, Virginia restocked elk in the Alleghanies. They thrived well enough to permit hunting for several seasons. Unlike the whitetail, however, the *wapiti* cannot coexist with small woodlots and agriculture, and its return to the Bay country is out of the question.

The Bay country has retained another big game animal, the black bear. Common in colonial days, it followed the pattern of the elk and vanished from most of its range. It kept a foothold in the Blue Ridge and Alleghanies and in the southeastern swamps; in Virginia enough remain to permit an annual hunting season. A few bears lingered in Maryland into the twentieth century, but there are none left in the upper Bay country and only an occasional stray in the mountains. Maryland has no open season. In Virginia the annual kill has risen from about 150 in the late 1930s to over 300. In 1967, the Dismal Swamp produced seven. One of the largest bears ever taken east of the Mississippi came from the Dismal Swamp in 1944. Its weight was estimated at over 700 pounds. Its skull measured 12½ inches in length and 31 inches in circumference. An average Virginia bear weighs 200–500 pounds.

A newborn bear cub is small, no bigger than a rabbit. Its weight will increase 2000 times as it reaches maturity. By comparison a deer grows to about 80 times its birth weight, a human 20 times. The cubs, usually numbering two but sometimes three and rarely four, are born during the mother's hibernation. In March or April, when the young are about two months old, the mother and cubs leave the den. Throughout the summer they remain together, and sometimes den together during the first winter. They cover a relatively small range, estimated at about five square miles.

species. On that basis a few hundred panther rugs and wolfskin robes each year started a downward spiral. The trend accelerated as the decimation of the deer herd reduced the carnivores' food supply. Ultimately these two factors wiped out the Bay's wolves and cougars. Deer, on the other hand, were originally so numerous that the Bay country could provide a harvest of 20,000 to 30,000 annually. The hungry settlers and their successors exceeded even this bag; the decreasing herd finally reached a nadir in the 1930s. A nucleus of deer remained and under intelligent management restocked the range. Virginia and Maryland game commissions now regulate the hunting season and bag limits to keep the annual harvest at an acceptable figure and so maintain the Bay deer herd close to the maximum stable density. No wolves or cougars remain, nor is there a desire to restock. Hence they have not come back in proportion to the deer herd, and the only animal that feeds on the whitetail is man.

The wolf and the cougar are gone, but their smaller relatives, the bobcat and the foxes, were never exterminated. Since these species are lower in the food web, the Bay country could support a larger biomass. With a smaller average weight, their populations numbered larger still. Mohr's figures indicate an original population of perhaps 5,000 foxes and half as many bobcats. Feeding on rabbits, squirrels, mice, and other small animals which have remained plentiful, they did not lose their food supply as did the larger carnivores. Hunting pressure has been less severe; additional red foxes were even imported and stocked. Originally only the gray fox inhabited the Bay country; the red fox ranged from Pennsylvania north and west. When run by hounds, the gray fox normally holes or trees after a shorter, less exciting chase than its red cousin. The English colonists loved the chase; by 1750 they had imported and released their British fox, *vulpes vulpes*, from Long Island south to Virginia. The imports apparently bred with the native red foxes. Their cubs not only thrived but extended their range. Preferring broken country to solid forest, they profited by the conversion of woods to fields. By 1850 red foxes had spread as far as Georgia, and today they range nearly to the Gulf of Mexico.

A few bobcats remain in the Dismal Swamp and along the lower James. Some individuals reach unusually large size; there is a 1967 record of a 37 pound bobcat from Isle of Wight County. The average individual weighs 15 to 30 pounds. The bobcat hunts mostly at night. One can spend hours in the woods without even a glimpse of its spotted reddish hide. Seton writes that, in a lifetime of field observation, he saw only "one living Bobcat until it was trapped or treed by Dogs." Tracks one may see; they resemble those of a house cat, but each impression is larger and they are spaced farther apart. They differ from dog or fox tracks because the cat's retractile claws do not make a mark; the canine's footprint shows four claw marks in each print.

The furbearers—otter, beaver, mink, weasel, and muskrat—have been important economically since colonial days. Figures are available, for example, for the last 200 years of sales of North American muskrat skins on the London fur market. In the last third of the eighteenth century, imports were about 75,000 annually. From 1800 to 1850 the annual average was over 400,000, rising the last half of the century to two and a half million and reaching ten million in 1914. Additional North American furs, of course, were sold in American and other markets. In 1922–23, a record year, the continent produced over 15 million muskrat skins. The number

Muskrat

has since dropped, but it is still high. In recent years Maryland trappers have sold more muskrat pelts than any other state except Louisiana. In 1965 their catch was nearly a quarter million pelts, slightly under Louisiana's and slightly more than Virginia's. Most Virginia and Maryland muskrat came from the Bay country, particularly from the extensive marshes of Dorchester County on Maryland's Eastern Shore. A good skin brings over a dollar today; during the fur boom of the 1920s the price rose as high as six dollars: in 1900 it was as low as ten cents.

In 1612 Captain Smith described the muskrat by its Indian name and placed it in its proper family: "Mussacus is a beast of the form and nature of our water rat, but many of them smell exceedingly strong of musk." Both the European water rat and the American muskrat belong to the vole family—microtinae—and are closely related to the meadow mouse rather than to the house mouse or the Norway rat. The voles generally live in the open and have short tails, small ears and blunt noses, as opposed to the muridae—the old world rats and mice—who commonly live

chiefly on fish; the mink is also a fish eater, but varies its diet with land mammals captured near the water. The weasel, a land rather than water dweller, feeds chiefly on rats, mice, and other small animals. Its occasional raids on chicken yards, together with the lack of a market for its pelt, have resulted in a yearlong open season on the weasel. In the 1920s Virginia paid a one dollar bounty on weasels. The Virginia assembly repealed the bounty on weasels and on hawks and crows in 1930, primarily not because it represented an unsound approach to conservation—which it was—but because much of the $300,000 paid in bounties was fraudulently claimed in return for chicken heads pilfered from hotel garbage cans.

An exotic furbearer from South America is the nutria, a newcomer to the Dorchester County marshes. Strictly speaking, nutria is the name for the animal's fur; the animal itself is the coypu, but nutria is in common use for both. The nutria first became established in the United States in Louisiana. About thirty years ago a few were kept in captivity on Avery Island 100 miles west of New Orleans in the bayou country. A storm broke their pen and they escaped into the surrounding marshes. With no natural enemies and no important diseases, their population exploded. Trappers take over a million annually without depleting the stock. Nutrias have since been released in Oregon as well as in Maryland. On the Eastern Shore they have thrived, although there is a question of undesirable competition with the muskrat. The nutria weighs four times as much as the muskrat, but otherwise resembles it. The tail is a point of difference; the muskrat's is flattened on both sides, the nutria's is round.

Three species of squirrels inhabit the woods of the Bay area—gray, fox, and flying squirrels. The fox squirrel prefers open woods or the wood border, either hardwood or conifers; the gray and flying squirrels prefer extensive stands of hardwoods but can adapt to city parks or tree-filled suburbs. The Bay lies outside the range of the red squirrel, inhabitant of coniferous forests farther inland and to the north. John Smith observed all three Chesapeake species, and wrote in 1624 of "Squirrels . . . near as great as our smallest sort of wild Rabbits, some blackish, or black and white, but most are gray. A small beast they have called *Assapanik*, but we call them flying Squirrels, because, spreading their legs, and so stretching the largeness of their skins that they have been seen to fly 30 or 40 yards."

Smith's blackish squirrel may have been a melanistic gray squirrel. This black phase occurs chiefly in the northern part of its range. Smith may have seen melanos in New England or may have seen one of the rarer black individuals of the Bay country. Perhaps he was thinking of the fox squirrel, which in the southeast has a blackish head with light gray markings. His rabbit-sized squirrel must have been the fox squirrel, which weighs up to three pounds. Flying squirrels, although occurring also in Asia and eastern Europe, were novelties to the English colonists. Graceful and attractive creatures then as now, an *assapanik* from Virginia even caught the royal eye of James I of England.

As Captain Smith suggested, gray squirrels were abundant. Ernest Thompson Seton estimated their population density at 1,000 per square mile, giving about one billion "as the lowest reasonable guess at the primitive number." On this basis the Bay country held perhaps five million. To the early farmer they were pests, destroying his corn and wheat. Seton notes that in 1749 Pennsylvania paid bounties on 640,000. He records hunts in Kentucky, New York, and Ohio bagging respectively 9,780, "upwards of 2,000," and 19,660 squirrels. An 1807 Ohio law required every citizen to turn in 100 scalps annually or pay a three-dollar fine.

Under such pressure the hordes vanished. Between 1895 and 1915 Seton visited every state in its original range without seeing a single gray squirrel outside a park or refuge. Like the passenger pigeon, the squirrel seemed destined for extinction. Conservation came too late for the pigeon, but it did bring back the squirrel. Common today in the parks and suburbs of the Bay area, the gray squirrel is also one of the most popular small game animals. The 1965–66 bag in Virginia, for example, averaged about 45 per square mile. On the assumption of one squirrel shot out of every five, the statewide population density averaged about 225 per square mile, just over 20 percent of Seton's estimate of the primitive number.

Unlike the gray, the fox squirrel and flying squirrel are rarely seen. The fox squirrel has always been far less numerous, and today is a rare resident of the Bay country, confined to the Eastern Shore. The Blackwater National Wildlife Refuge in Dorchester County harbors much of the remaining population. Eastern Shore hunters, for unknown reasons, call them "gray squirrels," and speak of gray squirrels as "cat squirrels."

The flying squirrel is much more common than its visible presence suggests. Small and nocturnal, it spends most of the daylight hours out of sight in a tree, attic, or bird house. John Bachman, the famous American naturalist, wrote in 1949 of a colony living in a martin house on top of a pole. The house had to be taken down. When it fell, the watcher saw "great numbers of flying squirrels, screech owls, and leather-winged bats running from it . . . 20 flying squirrels . . . and as many bats, and we know there were six screech owls."

As numerous as the flying squirrel, the chipmunk is better known because it prefers the day as much as the flying squirrel prefers the night. In the Bay area, as elsewhere in its range, the chipmunk chooses woodland borders, outbuildings, woodpiles, and brushy fields for its territory. One rarely sees chipmunks in unbroken forests or in cultivated fields. Although it can climb trees, it makes or finds an underground burrow and rarely strays far from it. In its burrow the chipmunk stores a winter food supply of nuts, seeds, and acorns, a habit responsible for its scientific name *tamias*, the

Opossum

Some opossum songs praise the taste of its meat:

> "Chicken is good, and 'taters are sweet,
>   And possum is very very fine,
> But give me, oh give me, I really wish you would
>   A watermelon hanging on a vine."

Others describe its appearance:

> "The coon he got a bushy tail
>   The possum's tail is bare
> The rabbit got no tail at all
>   Just a little bunch of hair."

Some are hunting songs:

> "Possum is a cunning thing
>   He rambles in the dark.
> Nothing at all disturbs his mind
>   But to hear my bulldog bark."

It is not surprising that, in the words of the song, nothing disturbs the possum's mind. He has a tiny brain; Seton found that the brain cavity of an opossum's skull could hold only 25 beans. Far more intelligent is the *Aroughcun*. Measuring the size of a raccoon's brain in the same way, Seton found it six times as big as the opossum's, holding 150 beans. The raccoon is as clever as the opossum is dull. A pet raccoon can uncover jars, turn doorknobs, and uncork bottles. In the wild it has the wit and speed to catch fish and frogs, locate a carefully covered nest of turtle eggs, or open a mussel shell.

Raccoons inhabit the Bay country from the Virginia Capes to the Susquehanna. Strictly nocturnal, one rarely sees a live raccoon unless it is treed by hounds. Like the opossum, raccoons often are killed by cars on the highways at night, and too frequently one sees a rumpled coonskin on the shoulder of a country road. Their tracks are plentiful along Bay beaches and river banks. The flatfooted prints suggest those of a small child; each

Raccoon

of the five toes leaves its mark in front of a flat palm. The front paw is half as big as the back, which may be four or five inches in length. The opossum's tracks are somewhat similar. They too show all five toes but are smaller and are about the same length front and back—about two inches.

The striped skunk is another nocturnal prowler rarely seen during the day. Its scent, however, after a successful nighttime encounter with a hound or a painful collision with a car, establishes it as a common resident of the Bay country. After one sniff, Captain Smith misidentified the skunk as the polecat, its malodorous European cousin, a species of marten. Opinions on the skunk's aroma vary among later naturalists. Seton found it, if very dilute, "rather agreeable," although he confesses that it resembles "a mixture of strong ammonia, essence of garlic, burning sulfur, a volume of sewer gas, a vitriol spray, a dash of perfume musk, all mixed together and intensified a thousand times." John Burroughs, the American nature writer, thought that "a good smeller will enjoy its most refined intensity . . . it is tonic and bracing." Less generous observers will tend to agree with Dr. C. Hart Merriam, first Chief of the U.S. Biological Survey, who cited the medicinal values of skunk musk but ended his discussion with a classic understatement: "It certainly deserves more extended trial; but, unfortunately, its offensive odor is a practical bar to its general employment."

In the animal world, the skunk possesses very nearly the ultimate weapon. Few of the Chesapeake carnivores will attack a skunk; even bears have been seen to clear the trail to let a skunk pass. The great horned owl, another night hunter, does prey on the skunk. Striking silently from above the owl can attack without warning and capture the skunk before it can defend itself. Horned owls are scarce in the Bay, however, and most Chesapeake skunks are immune to natural enemies. Man takes his toll, both on the highway and with traps. Neither Maryland nor Virginia protects the skunk, and some thousand pelts find their way annually to the fur markets. The popularity of this type of fur has decreased, however, for obvious reasons, and the Bay skunks are more than holding their own. They have recently spread to the lower Eastern Shore to complete their conquest of the Chesapeake.

The woodchuck, or groundhog, common elsewhere in Maryland and Virginia, is scarce in the Bay country. As a site for its burrow it prefers rocks and hills to the flat sandy soil of the Tidewater. The largest North American member of the squirrel family, the groundhog is a squat, brownish marmot with a flattened tail and strong claws. A vegetarian, its taste for garden crops and its holes in fields and pastures make the woodchuck unpopular with farmers. State laws permit a continuous open season and 'chuck shooting with rifle and scope is popular among marksmen. With few natural enemies, however, the groundhog thrives without protection. Our only animal honored by a day in the calendar, the groundhog is supposed to predict the weather every February 2. Most 'chucks, in fact, are still hibernating on Groundhog Day and do not cast a shadow until sometime in March.

Of America's mammals the bats are probably the least familiar to the layman and even to the amateur naturalist. Largely nocturnal in habits, they are difficult to spot and observe, and even more difficult to identify by species. It is surprising to learn that North America supports 38 distinct species of bats, over ten percent of the total number of mammal species on the continent. In the Bay country, at one time of the year or another, one may find nine species: little brown Myotis, Keen Myotis, Eastern pipistrel, and the big brown, evening, silver-haired, hoary, red, and Eastern big-eared bats. They differ little in size, with wingspans ranging from five inches for the pipistrel up to eight for the red bat and the big brown bat. In color they vary from brick red through brown to blackish. The myotes hibernate; most of the others migrate south when cold weather eliminates the insects on which they feed. Most species spend their days in hollow trees, in caves, or abandoned buildings, but the red and hoary bats sleep in the woods, hanging from twigs. One species has, as its name suggests, grotesquely enlarged ears. Despite these and other differences, it is virtually impossible to tell one species from the other as they flit through the dusk. Should one desire to identify an individual bat he needs a specimen in one hand and a guide in the other. Even then, Dr. Burt suggests that doubtful cases be sent to a museum. Valueless as game, lacking the color and appeal of birds, ugly in appearance, and difficult to watch, bats are unlikely to lose their traditional air of mystery.

Completing the list of Chesapeake fauna are a variety of mice, voles, shrews, moles and other small creatures that inhabit the woods, fields, and marshes of the Bay country. Near the bottom of the food chain, these animals make up for their small size by their vast numbers. Mohr estimates the biomass of the short-tailed shrew, for example, at about 5,000 pounds per square mile. At a weight of about one ounce, this figure implies a population of close to 100,000 per square mile or 150 per acre. The small animals come in great variety as well as great numbers. Perhaps the large number of individuals increases the probability of mutations leading to the evolution of new species. In the State of Virginia, for example, one can find nine species of shrews and twenty species of rats and mice. Small mammals seem to react more readily to their environment than large mammals and thus increase the number of distinct species. North America supports about 250 species of small mammals and seven species of deer. The kangaroo rat has been identified as 18 separate species; an area one hundred miles in diameter might include specimens of half of these, each slightly modified according to the ecology of its particular range. At the other extreme, the puma exists as a single species whether it inhabits the Florida Everglades or the New Mexico rimrock, and the black bear of the Dismal Swamp is the same species as the "cinnamon bear" of British Columbia.

The Bay country's small mammals belong to one of two orders: insectivores in the case of moles and shrews, rodents in the case of rats and mice. The Chesapeake fauna include the common and starnosed mole and five shrews—Fisher's, little and large short-tailed, Dismal Swamp, and Carolina blarina. There are four general groups of native mice: harvest mice, white-footed mice, voles, and jumping mice; one native rat, the swamp rice rat, as well as those unwelcome immigrants from the Old World, the Norway rat and the house mouse.

The large size of these populations, together with their fecundity (a meadow mouse may have four litters of six every season), underline the ecological importance of the higher order consumers—snakes, hawks, foxes, and other so-called predators. Mohr's 150 mice per acre exist despite a proportional biomass of mice-eaters. If man were to eliminate all predators, as misguided game managers believed desirable fifty years ago, the rodents could take over the out-of-doors. The balance of nature is delicate, delicate to an extent that scientists are only today coming to realize. Many ecological relationships are more subtle than the obvious link between rodent and hawk. Mankind must quickly come to understand them, lest we upset nature's balance, perhaps irreversibly, and add to the damage we have already wrought on our environment.

IX

Chesapeake Bay Reptiles

AT THE HEAD of many a Bay creek lies the wreck of a dredge boat, her decks fallen in, planks parted from the stem, awash in the brackish tidal water. Like as not she is the home of a dozen painted turtles. Some float between the rotted frames, heads protruding an inch out of water. Others sun themselves on the deck. A handsome species, the shell is black on top and salmon-colored beneath. They are surprisingly alert for creatures whose lack of speed is proverbial; try to row quietly up to the wreck and every head disappears, every turtle scuttles off the sunbaked deck with a splash. If one beaches his boat on a grassy shore alongside the hulk, he may find another species, the round-shelled, dull-colored mud turtle. A scavenger, it noses along the water's edge for dead fish and crabs. On the steep, wooded bank rising from the creek the box tortoise rustles in the dry leaves, searching for worms, grubs, and berries. In all, the Bay and its shores harbor twenty-one different species of turtles, tortoises, and terrapins.

Although the three names are used interchangeably, the term tortoise, from the Middle English word *tortuce*, generally indicates a land animal; turtle, from the Spanish *tortuga*, a sea or water dweller; and terrapin, from its Algonquin Indian name, the diamondback of the Atlantic coast. The box tortoise is the reptile one often sees crossing a country road, particularly after a heavy rain. One wonders how so slow a creature survives the network of roads in this automotive age. Natural longevity helps; they have been known to live for a full century. Their brown or brownish-yellow shell is about five inches long. The male is larger than the female and his coloring is more showy. His legs are plated with scales of bright yellow; his eyes are red. The female is brown-eyed and generally more subdued in coloring and behavior. A creature of the dry woods, the box tortoise can swim if he must. If he finds a vegetable garden he varies his diet of insects with nibbles of tomatoes and strawberries.

The snapping turtle inhabits creeks and rivers and grows to as much as 90 pounds with a shell measuring 18 inches across. Wary in the water, a captured snapper lives up to his name. Turtles with large shells seem to have mild tempers; those with small shells are fierce. The snapper is in the latter category. His tail, legs, and neck are much longer and heavier in proportion to his shell than those of the box tortoise, and he thrashes about, snapping and twisting, when picked up. The best way to carry a snapper

Snapper

is by the tail, with caution. Countrymen maintain that when he bites, he holds on until sundown. No picky feeder, the snapper can be fattened for the table in the family garbage can. The snapper spends the winter in the mud or in a hole in a stream bank. In March he emerges to spend the summer feeding on fish, crabs, and an occasion waterfowl. The female snapper lays up to 80 eggs; these are eaten raw by raccoons and fried by watermen. The rivers of the Bay support a substantial commercial catch. With pots, trotlines, handlines, and dip nets, Maryland watermen took over a quarter million pounds in 1957 and in 1958. They brought a market value of $28,000.

Other Bay turtles are the Florida cooter, the stinkpot, and the spotted, map, and red-bellied turtles. Near the Capes one occasionally finds sea turtles—greens, loggerheads, leatherbacks, and hawkbills. Systematic hunting in the Caribbean has reduced their numbers and they are seen less and less frequently. Sometimes these visitors from warmer seas are trapped in the Chesapeake in the autumn. Unable to find their way back to the ocean and not adapted to the cold, they die before spring.

Best known of the Chesapeake's turtles is the diamondback terrapin. Over the years the public's taste for terrapin has varied. In 1797 a Maryland law forbade feeding terrapin to slaves more often then twice each week. Its humanitarian purpose was to protect the slaves from an unvarying diet of these abundant and easily taken turtles. A century later diamondback became a delicacy; between 1870 and 1900 schooner-rigged terrapin smacks took as much as 80,000 pounds annually, reducing the stock to near extinction. In 1917, at the peak of the market, a dozen brought $128. The last fifty years have seen a slow increase in their numbers, with an annual catch of about 10,000 pounds in recent years and a price that fluctuates widely from year to year. The demand today is not very great; terrapin is a delicacy known to only a few gourmets. A few enterprises raise them commercially in pens and ponds; there is one near Crisfield on Maryland's Eastern Shore. Others are taken in pound nets, scrapes, dredges, tongs, and haul seines. The turtle scrape consists of a net trailing from two rigid metal hoops dragged by a bridle. Unlike the dredge, it has no teeth and does not dig into the mud; the terrapin is caught as he swims near the bottom.

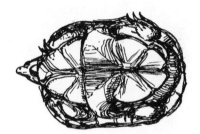

Box Tortoise   Diamondback Terrapin

Mud Turtle

The diamondback's shell may reach nine inches in length; females are generally larger than males. An eight-inch terrapin weighs a pound or more. On its diet of crustaceans and mullusks it may live for 40 years. Eggs from a single mating remain fertile for two or three years. The female deposits them, from half a dozen to 25 or more, near the water; they hatch in 90 days.

About 30 species of snakes inhabit the Bay area, most harmless, a few poisonous. Rattlesnakes, scarce on the Atlantic Coastal Plain, seldom occur near the Chesapeake. Occasional coral snakes have been reported in the pine woods south of Norfolk. Less dangerous but more common is the water moccasin or cottonmouth. Authorities maintain that the cotton-mouth, a native of southern Virginia, does not occur north of the Potomac. Most Maryland "moccasins" are actually misidentified black water snakes. Their difference in behaviour is a good way to distinguish the two species: the water snake is more timid, but the moccasin is apt to hold its ground, vibrate its tail, rear its head, and bare its fangs. On close inspection of a moccasin, the careful observer can see the characteristics common to all pit vipers—the pit between nostril and eye, elliptical pupils, fangs extending downward from the roof of the mouth, and continuous bands of scales under the tail.

The copperhead, another pit viper, inhabits the entire Bay area except the low marshes of the Eastern Shore. The most common poisonous snake, it is shy and retiring. Despite its abundance there are few records of copperhead bites. Handsomely marked, the copperhead is a rich reddish-brown with darker hourglass markings. The longest known copperhead measured fifty-three inches; they rarely exceed three feet and most are smaller. Like the cottonmouth, the copperhead resembles several non-poisonous snakes including the milk snake, hognose snake, red rat snake, and water snake. Copperheads hibernate during the winter. Mating occurs in May and the young are born, complete with fangs and poison, in October. Small mammals, insects, birds, and frogs make up the copperhead's diet. The snake strikes its victim, holding it until the venom takes effect, then swallows it headfirst.

The Chesapeake reptiles, though of little direct economic importance, play their parts in the food chains and the balance of nature of the Tide-water. Snakes like the blacksnake are efficient predators and share in the control of rodents. They do not deserve the indiscriminant slaughter often meted out to them. Turtles, with the possible exception of snappers and stinkpots, bring joy to young boys as pets. Painted turtles and redbellies have been caught for food in the past, but are of little economic impor-tance now. All the reptiles, whether the water snake swimming along the wild rice and tuckahoe weeds or the painted turtle floating motionless beside the ruins of a dock, add life and their own form of beauty to the Tidewater area.

X

British Warships on the Bay

THE WAR OF 1812 brought more fighting to the Chesapeake than any other war. Ironically, it yielded fewer results. Three issues had impelled President Madison's administration to declare war: "Free Trade," "Sailors' Rights," and rivalry for a western empire. The last was a legacy from the War of Independence accentuated by a new nationalism; the first two an outgrowth of Britain's struggle to bring down Napoleon.

Outside supplies were essential to both France and Britain. The United States, as the largest neutral supplier, was anxious to provide them. Each belligerent waged economic warfare on the other. Britain issued Orders in Council for a blockade of the entire European continent and deployed her navy to enforce it. Americans wanted to maintain their profitable exports and resented any curtailment of "Free Trade." Feeling was greatest in the southern states whose agricultural exports were their main livelihood. Restoration of "Free Trade" became the slogan of Madison's Republican party.

The issue of "Sailors' Rights" grew directly out of the blockade, a task which demanded a huge navy. The British ensign flew from 150 ships of the line, 164 frigates, 134 sloops, and over 500 smaller warships. Manning the fleet was a continuing problem requiring the press gang for a steady supply of seamen. Royal Navy captains insisted on the right to stop and search any ship—British or American—inspect the crews, and take off supposed deserters. To escape the harsh, dangerous life of His Majesty's service many a British sailor had jumped ship and signed on a better paying American merchantman. Some had been able to obtain "protections," papers falsely identifying them as American citizens immune from the press gang. To the recapture of deserters the United States could hardly object, but shorthanded British captains impressed bona fide American seamen as well. President Madison reported to an angry Congress that 2273 Americans had been forced into the Royal Navy between 1803 and 1806. Life below decks was hard. Sympathy for illegally impressed seamen as well as the affront to national honor added "Sailors' Rights" to the Republican battle cry.

89

Commissioned by President Madison to negotiate with the British government, James Monroe and William Pinckney protested frequently and forcefully. In June, 1812, after six years of discussion, a favorable turn in Britain's fortunes of war permitted the Prime Minister to lift the blockade. But in another of history's ironies the United States, lacking rapid transatlantic communications, declared war two days later.

Old Cape Henry Light

Hostilities began on the Great Lakes in the summer of 1812 but did not reach the Chesapeake until late the following winter, when the failure of Napoleon's Russian campaign allowed the British to divert forces across the Atlantic. Embarrassed by the successes of American frigates in single ship engagements with Royal Navy craft and hoping to relieve American pressure on Canada, the admiralty transferred "ships from other important services . . . to bring the naval war to a termination, either by the capture of American national vessels, or by strictly blockading them in their own waters." Admiral Sir John Warren, Commander in Chief of the North American and West Indian Stations, complied by ordering a blockade of the United States from New York southward. Capitalizing on New England's dislike for "Mr. Madison's War," he left the northern ports free to continue their trade with the enemy—lucrative for Yankee merchants and essential to continuation of British campaigns in Europe. Sir John ordered into the Bay his second in command, Rear Admiral Sir George Cockburn, with a fleet of four ships of the line and eight smaller war vessels. On board was Colonel Sir Sidney Beckwith with 1800 troops, redcoated army regulars and Royal Marines plus two greenclad companies of *Chasseurs*. French soldiers recruited from prisoner of war camps for garrison duty in the West Indies, they were called *Chasseurs Britanniques*, or, to raise hopes of later service in a cooler, healthier climate than the Caribbean, *Chasseurs Canadiens*.

In February, 1813, the force anchored in Lynnhaven Bay and began the Chesapeake campaign. The same waterways that helped the colonists to settle in Tidewater were to serve equally well in carrying the war to their descendants.

Admiral Cockburn immediately made a reputation for himself. In the opinion of Maryland historian Francis F. Beirne, he became "the most feared and hated of all His Majesty's officers on service in America." One of his subalterns, Lieutenant Gleis, described Sir George's tactics:

> Whenever a favorable opportunity presented itself, parties landed, plundered or destroyed government stores, and brought off all shipping that could be reached. In a word, hostilities carried on in the Chesapeake resembled the expeditions of ancient Danes against Great Britain rather than modern war between civilized nations.

For two months the British harassed the Lynnhaven area. The troops commandeered livestock and supplies to replenish their stores, burned an occasional farmhouse, and waged psychological warfare through the farmers' slaves. To some he gave arms with the suggestion that they use them to gain freedom from their masters. To others he promised freedom if they came on board the ships of his fleet. Some slaves reached the ships. According to American accounts, possibly more emotional than true, the heartless and hypocritical Cockburn reneged on his promise and sold them, to his own profit, in the West Indies slave markets.

The Admiral reconnoitered Norfolk but decided temporarily to by-pass it. In April he stood up the Chesapeake opposed chiefly by the Secretary of the Treasury who ordered all navigational lights extinguished. The fleet captured the Baltimore privateer *Dolphin* and three armed schooners in the mouth of the Rappahannock, feinted at Baltimore, then sacked Frenchtown on the Elk River and Havre de Grace on the Susquehanna. Cockburn made good use of his new "secret weapon," the Congreve rocket, an incendiary which could set fire to a city from a range of several miles. Ashore the landing parties faced only militia, who proved completely inadequate against regular troops. One artillery unit, sighting British boats approaching their battery, shot all their ammunition before the boats came within range, then abandoned the position. At Havre de Grace the militia commander was conveniently absent from his post when the assault began. Except for two men, the infantry and artillerymen took to the woods. Philip Albert and John O'Neil held their ground, working the guns against Cockburn's entire fleet. A British landing force assaulted the battery at bayonet point and Albert, too, fled. O'Neil, an elderly Irishman, was injured by the recoil of one of his pieces, and the redcoats captured him with a musket in each hand, shouting at his fellow militiamen to come back and fight. Impressed by the old man's valor, Sir George held him as prisoner for several days and then released him. Later, on learning O'Neil's nationality, Cockburn avowed that his fate should have been far worse. The city fathers of Philadelphia, recognizing O'Neil's uncommon pluck, awarded him a ceremonial sword.

From the Susquehanna Admiral Cockburn crossed the Bay and stood up the Sassafras, where he overcame the defenses of Fredericktown and Georgetown and burned them both. On June 1 Admiral Warren entered the Bay, and Cockburn rendezvoused with him for an attack on Norfolk. The combined flotilla included eight ships of the line, 12 frigates, and many smaller vessels. The Norfolk defenders skirmished on June 19 with British frigates in the Roads. At sunrise on June 22 came the main assault. Embarking from 14 men of war anchored in the lower James between Newport News and Pig Point, an amphibious force of 4000 sailors, marines, and soldiers began the attack. One group landed near Craney Island, but a second group was repulsed before the boats reached shore. Facing determined, organized opposition, Admiral Warren reembarked all his troops and chose a softer target. Hampton, across the James, was a smaller prize but lacked effective defenses. On the 25th the British routed the defending militia and occupied the town. The troops, led by the *Chasseurs*, got out of hand. According to Lieutenant Colonel Charles Napier, one of the brigade commanders, "every horror was committed with impunity, rape, murder, pillage." American protests brought on an investigation, and Colonel Beckwith determined that atrocities had been committed but chiefly by the *Chasseurs*. Warren detached them from duty in the Chesapeake and sent them to Canada, where upon landing in Halifax they started a riot. Eventually they were shipped back to England and out of the service.

Leaving Hampton, Cockburn with seven ships of the line, seven frigates, and 11 smaller craft sailed north again and entered the Potomac. Washington and Alexandria were alarmed, and Congress considered forming itself into a military company to defend the capital. This stouthearted proposal came to naught, however, and Washington was spared for a year when Cockburn's fleet turned downriver at the narrows where Dahlgren now stands.

Early in the summer, incredibly enough, American vessels had been selling provisions and water to Cockburn's fleet. In the Chesapeake as in New England some Americans were willing to traffic with the enemy at a suitable price. Now the Secretary of Navy and the War Department issued orders to seize any such vessels. The British force was able to commandeer the stores it needed, however, and they kept the Tidewater in continuous turmoil. Cockburn claimed that his men, no wanton looters, paid market price for the provisions and livestock taken. Where there was no resistance, he said, there was no destruction. Marylanders and Virginians disagreed and drank to the early death of this "pirate, a notorious freebooter." Sir George was not insensitive to criticism in American journals. Later, when his troops captured Washington, he personally supervised the destruction of the city's printing presses. It is said that he took particular care that type with the letter "c" was thrown into the flames so that the Yankee writers could not insult him again. American toasts notwithstanding, Cockburn survived the war, but his favorite nephew was killed in a raid on an Eastern Shore village. Hearing of the youth's death, the Admiral growled, "He was worth more than the whole damned town." During the summer Sir George took over 129 prizes. In September, temporarily satisfied with his accomplishments, he left the Bay and headed south to harass the coasts of Georgia and the Carolinas.

Two factors influenced the British to mount a strong attack on the United States territory the following spring. Successes on the Continent had brought about Napoleon's exile to Elba by the end of March, freeing resources for the American theater. British reverses in Canada, moreover, called for retaliation. The Americans had burned the towns of York, Newark, and St. David. Irritation at this setback was aggravated by the increased losses at sea to American privateers. Captain Thomas Boyle, master of a Baltimore raider, even presumed to inform Lloyd's of London that his ship had established a blockade of the British Isles. Major General Robert Ross with a force of Wellington's veterans was dispatched to Bermuda. There they boarded ships of Vice Admiral Sir Inglis Cochrane, new Commander in Chief of the North American Station. Admiral Cochrane was anxious to meet the Americans and had it "much to heart to give them a complete drubbing." In particular he intended to capture Baltimore, the only major city on the Atlantic coast never held by a foreign enemy. In August with 21 men of war and 4000 troops he joined Admiral Cockburn who had reentered the Bay in March. On the 15th the combined force anchored at the mouth of the Potomac where Cochrane, Cockburn, and Ross held a council of war.

The British knew that their only opposition afloat was Commodore Joshua Barney's small flotilla of one schooner and 13 armed barges manned by 500 men. Bottled up in the Patuxent with H.M.S. *Loire* to keep him there, Barney posed little threat. At Cockburn's suggestion, Cochrane ordered a sweep up the Patuxent to destroy the barges followed by an overland attack on Washington. The plan succeeded. The fleet sailed up the Patuxent to Benedict and were spared the inconvenience of fighting Barney's gunboats when he destroyed them himself, moving men and guns to Bladensburg to add to the defenses of Washington. At Benedict General Ross landed his troops without a shot and on March 20 set out towards Upper Marlboro, Bladensburg, and Washington. The Battle of Bladensburg, contemptuously dubbed the "Bladensburg Races," fortunately does not belong to the history of the Bay. Except for Barney's sailors, the numerically superior Americans under General Winder were routed. On the evening of the battle, August 24, the British were in Washington and the city was in flames. On the night of the 25th the invaders abandoned the city; on the 29th they reembarked at Benedict. Further humiliation awaited the national capital. On August 27 a seven-ship British squadron had ascended the Potomac under the command of Commodore Gordon. At Fort Washington, constructed on the Maryland shore below the city to meet just such an attack, the American commander sighted the ships, destroyed the fort, and fled without firing a shot. Gordon sailed upriver to Alexandria, burned one vessel and loaded others with commandeered flour, cotton, and tobacco. On September 1 he stood downriver with his prizes, safely passed the American batteries at White House and Indian Head, and regained the Bay.

Meanwhile, Cochrane had lost one of his senior officers, Sir Peter Parker, commander of the force blockading Baltimore. Parker received orders home, but decided that he wanted "one more frolic with the Yankees." He set out on a raid on the Eastern Shore and was killed by a load of Yankee buckshot. His body having been sent home preserved in Jamaica rum, Sir Peter became the subject of three poems. Lord Byron, his cousin, wrote an eulogy. A less sympathetic Republican poet, Phillip Frenau, wrote a piece entitled "Sir Peter Petrified." A third poet, unknown and irreverent, composed a ballad which ended:

> So not in fun
> To be outdone
> They sent this gallant sparker,
> Well seasoned, home
> In his favorite rum—
> The far-famed Peter Parker.

Now free to strike his primary objective, Cochrane determined to "make a demonstration upon the City of Baltimore, which might be converted into a real attack should circumstances appear to justify it." On September 11 the fleet entered the Patapsco and on the 12th landed troops. The first day's battle was nearly a repeat of Bladensburg, but the Americans retreated to well prepared defenses which had been lacking at Washington. On the 13th the Admiral's bomb ketches closed on Fort McHenry and began a 25-hour-long attack. When the dawn's early light on the 14th revealed the Stars and Stripes still flying, Admiral Cochrane decided to settle for a demonstration rather than a real attack. General Ross had been killed and his second in command led the troops back on board the fleet. Without harassing Tidewater further, Cochrane left the Bay to prepare for his next operation, the attack on New Orleans.

Most Americans, when they think of it at all, consider the War of 1812 a victory for the United States, a concluding chapter of the American Revolution. In fact, however, neither Baltimore nor any other American battlefield brought an end to hostilities. Just as European rivalries caused the American war, so peace in the New World awaited the end of the conflict in the Old. Britain's victory over Napoleon had eliminated the need for a blockade and she withdrew her Orders in Council which had established it. Without the farflung blockade to maintain, a smaller Royal Navy could man its ships without impressing American seamen. Although Britain was unwilling to write either of these concessions into the peace treaty, the American negotiators realized that the issues of blockade and impressment had tacitly been resolved, at least for the moment. This accomplished, the Americans could consider compromising the remaining issues. To the British, who to this day do not dignify the war with a name of its own, only ancillary national interests had been involved in North America. It was on the Continent that their vital interests had been at stake. Once these had been secured by the defeat of Napoleon, the British negotiators too were disposed to compromise. In the end, both countries accepted the territorial division on the basis of *status quo ante bellum*, deferring other points for resolution after the peace treaty. Thus it was that the negotiators on Christmas Eve of 1814 signed the Treaty of Ghent, a document silent on the issues for which men had died from Canada to the Gulf of Mexico. In a final irony, the six weeks following the signing of the treaty saw two more bloody battles, a British victory at Mobile Bay and an American one at New Orleans.

The succeeding one hundred years were relatively peaceful for most of the world, "and within that peace the United States was safe and grew strong," writes historian Herbert Agar. "It was not the little war against England which won for America the blessing of being left alone, it was the enormous war against . . . Napoleon." For the United States, then, the chief result of the War of 1812 was a new unity based on national pride.

XI

Irregulars, Privateers, Slavers, and Poachers

IN 1700 THE citizens of Hampton, Virginia, complained to the royal governor concerning the drunk and inefficient Captain Aldred, captain of the guard ship and pirate chaser *Essex-Prize*. His ship was always far distant from the scene of action or out of commission when his services were needed. Some two hundred years later, complaints of a similar sort were made against the captain of one of the boats of the Maryland State Oyster Police Force. His reply, it is said, was that he had bought a substitute for the draft in the Civil War and had far too much regard for his skin to risk it in combat with oyster pirates.

The first man convicted of piracy in the Chesapeake was one of Claiborne's followers from Kent Island, convicted in the 1640s by Lord Baltimore's court in St. Marys. His crime was probably more a case of trespassing than genuine piracy. The line between legitimate trading, smuggling, privateering, and piracy was vague in the far reaches of empire in the 17th and 18th centuries. Continual war between England and her imperial and commercial rivals accounts for the lack of control and general lawlessness. Privateers, finding no honest employment in the infrequent periods of peace, often turned to piracy.

Englishmen, as well as Frenchmen and Spaniards, preyed on shipping leaving the Chesapeake. Occasionally they ventured into the Bay itself. The body of one French pirate was on display for several years, hanging in chains at Bloody Point on Kent Island. He had been caught in Norfolk wearing the silver buckles of one of his victims. An unusual reversal occurred when two retired pirates bought respectability and protection from a governor of Virginia by contributing to the endowment of William and Mary College. They had not made their fortunes on the Bay, however, but in foreign waters. Another royal governor, Spotswood, was so zealous in the suppression of piracy that the surviving pirates vowed vengeance if he ever ventured into the open sea. It is said he delayed a trip to England on this account. It was he who strengthened the naval patrols in the

Chesapeake and fortified the mouths of the James, York, and Rappahannock Rivers. Spotswood dispatched the expedition that killed Bluebeard in Albemarle Sound.

There were few English pirates of importance after 1730, but French, Spanish, and Dutch privateers caused such damage that guard ships were maintained in the Chesapeake, and the tobacco fleet sailed for England in an annual convoy sometimes numbering as many as two hundred ships. These assembled in Lynnhaven Roads inside Cape Henry for the long, slow voyage to England. During the wars, privateers from the Chesapeake, owned and manned by colonials, preyed on the Spanish and French commerce of the Caribbean, thus gaining experience that would make Baltimore the leading privateer port in later wars.

The southern end of the Chesapeake was the scene of irregular warfare during most of the Revolutionary War. Governor Dunmore, Virginia's last royal governor, fled to the Eastern Shore to join the considerable numbers of Loyalists there. Rival militia companies, Loyalist and Patriot, were formed. The Committee of Public Safety of Maryland, a Patriot organization, sent out its militia to demonstrate and cow the Tories. Proclamations against the Loyalists who would not take loyalty oaths threatened fines, imprisonment, and banishment. The Committee confiscated property and jailed several hundred Tories on the Eastern Shore. Nevertheless the Tories were able to conduct a waterborne guerrilla campaign from their unsuspected shore bases among their patriot neighbors.

The Council of Safety and the Committee of Observation, Patriot governing bodies, fitted out the *Defense*, 22 six-pounders, under Capt. Nicholson, to cruise against the Refugees. Two brigs, a sloop, and a dozen barges and galleys were also commissioned for the Chesapeake by Maryland authorities. Loyalists continued to operate from the Eastern Shore until the end of the war, some of the greatest activity being from 1781 to 1783 after the British defeat at Yorktown. The numerous small islands and marshes of Somerset and Worcester Counties provided secure havens for the Tories, who sometimes raided as far north as Eastern Bay.

In 1783, Governor Paca wrote to the Merchants of Baltimore:

> You cannot be strangers to the depredations daily committed by the enemy in our Bay. Not content with interrupting our trade, they are guilty of the most wanton destruction of property on the shores . . . From the best information we can obtain, there are twelve barges, one sloop, and two schooners belonging to the enemy, now in the Bay.

Paca asked for money to arm vessels. These, he wrote, "added to the *Polecat*, which we expect will be quite sufficient to drive them from the Bay." This force captured the Tory camp on Devil's (Deal) Island where they destroyed a number of barges. The final battle, and the bloodiest, was on November 30, 1783. Three of the Maryland barges attacked those of the Loyalists. Sixty-five of the seventy-five Tories in the fight were casualties; among the killed was the enemy leader.

Baltimore privateering began as early as 1775 in the Revolutionary War. The Council of Safety set up a prize court and began issuing letters of marque before the new nation had issued its Declaration of Independence. In seven years of war, two hundred and forty-eight vessels left the Chesapeake carrying letters of marque and reprisal. These ships were financed not only by Americans; French, Spanish, and Dutch merchants sent money to Baltimore to invest in her fast privateers. Carrying on the average from 12 to 16 guns, they bore such names as *Black Prince, Revenge, Buckskin Hero, Snake, Baltimore Hero, Ranger, Hercules, Delight, Willing Lass, Venus, Favorite*, and for a change of pace, *Molly*. They were very successful, capturing three hundred and forty ships in 1776 alone. British marine insurance rates rose £25; in the Channel itself in 1777 between Dover and Calais rates rose an additional ten percent. The recapture of American prizes became a secondary industry for some British ports which sent out their own privateers.

American privateers occasionally were in action before even clearing the Bay, fighting several engagements with the Loyalist barges. In one bloody battle barges from St. Georges Island at the mouth of the Potomac attacked a privateer from Alexandria. Though it was the victor, the privateer lost so many men it put back to Alexandria. Joshua Barney, who was to render valiant service in the same waters in the War of 1812, won a reputation in fights against Loyalists and as a privateersman. The British bestowed the expected honor upon Baltimore, naming that port "a nest of pirates."

In the 1790s, though this country was at peace, privateers continued to sail from Baltimore. Citizen Genêt, the ambassador of Republican France, arrived in the United States in 1793. To the surprise and embarrassment of the Federalist administration, he issued letters of marque authorizing the seizure of British shipping. French consuls in the United States set up prize courts for the condemnation and sale of the captured vessels. Merchants and seamen from Charleston and Philadelphia took advantage of this unusual opportunity, but Baltimore, home port of over 40 privateers, sailed the most raiders. Genêt's unorthodox activities eventually led to the United States Government's declaring him *persona non grata*, but the privateers continued to operate while France and England remained at war. Despite the irregularity of the captures, British owners had little success in recovering their property in American courts.

During the War of 1812, the Bay again sent out privateers and again was visited by the British, who established themselves on island bases for raids up and down the Chesapeake. British ships had been actively operating in the Bay well before the war began. In 1807 they blockaded French vessels in Annapolis harbor, and British vessels regularly anchored in Lynnhaven Roads with scant concern for American sovereignty on territorial waters. The ultimate indignity was the attack on the United States ship *Chesapeake*. Occasionally the British sent landing parties ashore to look for deserters. One such party in Annapolis was itself captured by the aroused citizenry, just as some fifty years earlier a press gang in Norfolk was captured by the angry townsmen.

Baltimore's privateers in the War of 1812 performed in the best traditions of that port. They were specialized vessels, fast and successful. The Eastern Shore ports of Oxford and Cambridge sent privateers to sea and Norfolk, at the height of the British blockade, slipped five vessels into the Atlantic.

During President Monroe's administration privateers under foreign flags sailed again from Baltimore. Their captains carried letters of marque from South American countries fighting their wars of liberation from Spain. Their was considerable sympathy for these efforts in the United States at the time, but presumably the interests of the privateersmen were mercenary. Both the Portuguese and Spanish ministers complained to Monroe that "whole squadrons of pirates were being fitted out in Baltimore." In all, perhaps twenty-five ships from Baltimore were in the business.

In addition to the legitimate craft that slid down their ways in the 1820s and 1830s, Maryland shipyards launched Baltimore clippers for the slave trade. Since slaving was illegal, owners wanted a fast ship—to avoid capture—and a cheap one—to cut financial losses if taken. A popular rig was the topsail schooner. Here fore-and-aft sails required only a few deckhands, and the square-rigged topsail added knots on the long run down the trades from Africa to Brazil or Cuba. Privateers too, for similar reasons, favored the Baltimore clipper. On the other side of the law, revenue cutters and men-of-war chose the same design for their fight against piracy, smuggling, and the slave trade.

About 1850 piracy in the form of oyster poaching returned to the Bay where it still lingers. Alarmed by the depletion of the beds in Delaware Bay and New England, Virginia and Maryland passed oyster conservation laws. Enforcing them was another matter. Poachers are ingenious and versatile, raiding private beds, oystering out of season, dredging on beds reserved for tonging, using power on days when sail is prescribed. Oysters, in the waterman's view, are a gift of God and outside the province of the states.

The Bay is large and conservation forces have sometimes been inadequate. Before 1865 sheriffs put out in private boats to pursue unlicensed oystermen. With the establishment of the Maryland State Oyster Police in 1868, two tenders and an armed steamer began regular patrols. Although funds were erratic, the fleet grew to two steam vessels and half a dozen schooners and bugeyes. In Virginia the State Militia was once called out to protect private beds. Private owners regularly man specially built watch towers. Skirmishes, including exchanges of large caliber gunfire, took place

Dredge Boat

between rival osytermen and between poachers and police. Tongers once mounted a cannon on shore to protect their beds from dredgers, and the police borrowed a cannon from the Naval Academy at Annapolis.

Despite criticism and lack of cooperation by the watermen, enforcement has become increasing effective. Today the patrol numbers over 100 craft supplemented by helicopters. Violence has decreased, but yawl boats sometimes give an illegal push to the dredgers, and poachers have been suspected of using ship-to-shore radio. The Bay retains something of its lawless past.

XII

The Estuarine System

AN ESTUARY is an arm of the sea where a river meets the ocean. The Chesapeake estuary is a complex of two major drowned river valleys, the Susquehanna and the Potomac, and as many as one hundred and fifty secondary estuaries formed by smaller rivers and creeks that enter the Bay. The unique features of estuaries result from the meeting of fresh and salt water and land and water. The environment varies a great deal in physical and chemical conditions. Tides alternately submerge and expose the shore and produce strong currents; great volumes of fresh water enter the system from the rivers; nutrients enter in great quantities through runoff; sediment is carried in by the ton; salinity varies from zero to that of the ocean. The shallow waters of the estuaries heat and cool rapidly, and temperature extremes in the Chesapeake are greater than those at sea. On the other hand, the waters of the Chesapeake are relatively protected from the waves and heavy surf of the sea. These conditions create opportunities and problems for the life in the Bay. Varied conditions produce many stresses and barriers to plant and animal life. A limited number of species, but great populations, are found; therefore, food chains are short and vulnerable without the usual alternate patterns. Besides the natural complexities of the environment, man has a strong impact on the system.

Water circulates in the Bay in a number of complex patterns. Tide, the earth's rotation, the influx of river water, depth and breadth of the body of water, meteorological factors, and seasonal variations affect the flow of water. Vertical mixing is caused by convection; horizontal cycling is produced by fresh surface water moving seaward while seawater flows up the Bay at greater depths.

In the shallow bays and tributary estuaries and in the narrower portions of the Chesapeake, currents are strong. The Current Tables show that a vessel can pick up as much as two knots in the middle of the Bay at the proper time. Spring tides, with sun and moon pulling together, may produce currents of three knots off Sandy Point, Maryland, a narrow section of the Chesapeake. In general, the tidal currents are stronger near the mouth of the Bay, decrease in the middle section, and increase again in the upper reaches. Weather may affect the tidal flow. Air pressure and wind can cause tides to rise three and, in extreme cases, six feet above normal in the upper Bay. The movements of great volumes of water as a result of meteorological factors may temporarily upset the normal patterns of water circulation.

Dorchester Marsh

The tidal effect is noticeable on the rivers as they flow slowly across the coastal plain. Far up the Pocomoke, the quiet dark stream seems remote from the open water and tides of the sea. Tall cypress trees shade its deep waters. Tuckahoe weeds and arrowroot add to the mood of a southern river far into the interior many miles from the sea. Rowing out from the bank, one soon discovers there are other forces acting on the boat besides the oars. A powerful tide carries one upstream against what would be the natural flow. Before the days of steam, such floods permitted oceangoing ships to work their way up the rivers of the Tidewater. They floated up with the flood, anchored or moored to the banks during the slack and ebb, and then were carried up again on the next flood. Thus all the Tidewater became directly accessible to ocean shipping.

Tide has important effects on the shores. It generates currents that erode shores and cut channels, at the same time depositing sand and sediment on existing bars. Twice daily it floods the lower beaches and salt marshes. The alternate wetting and drying, the accompanying temperature changes and exposure to winds and sunlight, and the mechanical effects of the currents create a rugged, ever-changing environment for the plants and animals of the intertidal zone. Tidal currents help mix fresh water from the rivers with salt water from the ocean, mingling their dissolved and suspended material. At each low tide in Baltimore, to consider one example, ten percent of the harbor water flows out to be replaced at high tide by an equal volume of Bay water. The amount of ebb equals the amount of flood, and the net change in volume is zero.

Superimposed on tidal circulation is the flow of the rivers in response to the earth's gravity. Nontidal circulation transports huge volumes of water, always to seaward. Of the mean total flow of 40,000 cubic feet per second, over half comes from the Susquehanna, the balance largely from the Potomac, Rappahannock, and James. Flow varies from year to year and from season to season. In February and March rain and melting snow normally increase the rate to a peak of 60,000 cubic feet per second. Fresh water tends to form a layer above the denser salt water. The nontidal current is fastest at the surface, slowest at the salt water interface.

In the Piedmont swift river waters scour and abrade banks and bottom, carrying loosened particles downstream as silt. Crossing the coastal plain

Western Shore Marsh

the rivers widen into estuaries and their velocity decreases. Under these conditions entrained silt particles begin to drop to the bottom, first the coarsest, heaviest particles and farther downstream the finer sediments. Most of the silt comes from the Potomac and the Susquehanna which annually dump into the Bay about 2,000,000 tons and 600,000 tons respectively. Most is deposited during the spring floods. Dams on the

Susquehanna keep much of its sediment in the river, but enough remains to make the upper Bay murky and its bottom muddy. Above Spesutie Island an average of one-third inch of sediment falls to the bottom every year. Before the river water reaches the lower Bay most of the particles have dropped, and the southern end has a sandier bottom. Part is alluvial fallout; part is sand washed in from coastal beaches. Marine scientists do not completely understand the physics of sedimentation and are studying its relationship to salinity.

Common Reed   Arrowhead Leaf   Reed

The currents thus help determine the environment of the Bay floor, which in turn determines the type of animals living there. Baymen are rightly concerned, then, with manmade changes in the Chesapeake watershed which can unexpectedly affect conditions far downstream and in the Chesapeake itself.

Besides solid matters physically borne along by moving waters, the Chesapeake contains salts in solution. The most plentiful is sodium chloride. Salinity varies seasonally and geographically. Lowest when spring rains and melting snow dilute the brackish Bay, it rises to a peak in late summer as river flow decreases and evaporation increases. Circulatory patterns of the Bay's water cause salinity to be highest at the Virginia Capes, decreasing steadily up the Bay and estuaries. In the Eastern Shore rivers, with small fresh water input and isolated from the Susquehanna's flow, salinity changes lag behind those of the Bay proper. Salinity differences act as barriers, creating distinct life zones for plants and animals. Oysters find optimum salinity in the middle section of the Chesapeake. The shipworm, as another example, is plentiful or absent depending upon high or low salinity.

Sea Walnuts

Bay waters also contain dissolved nutrients—nitrogen, phosphorus, and calcium—which enter the tributaries via runoff from the land. Sewer outfalls inject additional nitrogen and phosphorus. Unlike salinity, nutrient concentrations are highest in the estuaries. Most of the nitrates come from the Susquehanna, particularly during the spring floods. The seasonal concentration tapers off until the end of summer when it has dropped to a fiftieth of its springtime maximum. The reduction is thought to be caused by plankton growth and by lower river flow. Part of the nitrogen remains in the Bay in a complicated "nitrogen cycle," passing continuously through successive forms, living and nonliving, organic and nonorganic. The remainder is carried to sea with the outward flow through the Capes. Phosphorus has a cycle of its own, while calcium is irreversibly locked up by the shellmaking activities of a myriad of mollusks.

Photosynthesis, the miracle on which all Bay life depends, involves another dissolved compound, carbon dioxide. Normally a gas, carbon dioxide enters the water by diffusion from the air, from decomposing organic material, and from respiration of marine animals. The sun's rays, everywhere reaching the bottom of the Chesapeake, provide the energy by which photosynthesis converts inert carbon dioxide into living plants, submerged aquatics and microscopic one-celled phytoplankton. Warm water and plentiful nutrients accelerate plankton growth. The summer

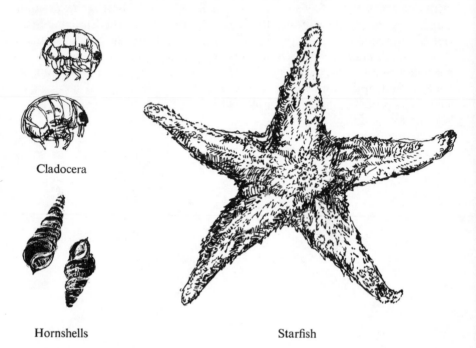

Cladocera

Hornshells   Starfish

crop makes the water cloudy, and some plankton "blooms" look as thick as pea soup. At the base of the Chesapeake's food pyramid, phyto- or plant plankton serve as food for zooplankton, minute larvae of marine animals. These in turn are preyed upon by the larger animals. The carnivores at the top of the marine food pyramid, like their terrestrial counterparts, are largest in size and fewest in numbers.

Both the microscopic phytoplankton and the larger marine grasses and seaweeds support Bay life in another way by producing the oxygen essential for respiration of marine animals. Additional oxygen is diffused from the air at the surface, especially in choppy seas. Conversely, sewage removes oxygen from solution through oxidation of organic matter. Water temperature also affects the amount of oxygen available, solubility being greatest in winter and lowest in summer. Warm water, by speeding the rate of animal respiration and of organic decay, causes faster use of an already reduced oxygen concentration. Further heating by thermal pollution reduces concentration to an even lower degree. In extreme cases, organic and thermal pollution can cause a near absence of oxygen. Such an "anaerobic" environment is deadly to fish, that require oxygen as do all other animals, and increasingly threatens the Bay's fisheries.

The peaceful surface of the Chesapeake hides a violent environment, a frontier between land, air, and sea. Life exists throughout its shallow waters. In contrast to the abyssal depths of the oceans, the Bay floor supports mollusks, worms, and crustaceans in great variety and numbers. Above the floor dwells an abundant animal population, both drifting and free swimming. The drifters are the larvae of fish, mollusks, comb jellies, and copepods. The swimmers are the fish that use the Bay as a spawning ground or as a permanent home. At the surface water birds prey on marine life. The Bay's ecology embraces many inputs, outputs, and cycles. Remarkably flexible, it can tolerate considerable change but is far from invulnerable. A greater knowledge of the system and control of man-made perturbations are essential for its preservation.

Ketch on Chesapeake Bay

XIII

Finfish and Fisheries of the Chesapeake

IN A SHALLOW estuary, varying conditions of depth, bottom, salinity, and concentrations of nutrients produce a number of distinct biological communities. The environment above the fall line is that of a freshwater stream; transition zones of brackish water are found further down river; at the mouth of the Bay the environment is marine. At the water's edge in the shallows, in the zone between tides, the life is quite different from the life at the bottom in one hundred feet of water in the center of the Chesapeake. The different conditions foster a varied assortment of fish: permanent residents, migrants, and occasional visitors. A rich source of mature fish, it is also vital as a nursery ground for countless millions of ocean fish.

Two hundred and two species have been recorded as permanent residents of the Chesapeake. There are four classes of migratory fish. The anadromous species such as shad, alewife, and striped bass, leave the marine environment to spawn in fresh water of the tributary rivers. The summer residents include hardhead, spot, and menhaden. Bluefish are migrants. In a class by itself is the American eel which leaves fresh and brackish water to spawn far at sea in the Atlantic.

The Bay harbors small catfish, juvenile flounders, stargazers which give an electric shock, stingrays that can cause a nasty wound, and timid sand sharks. There are weird and grotesque species like the toadfish, pipefish, halfbeak, and goby. In the creeks and rivers at the head of the Bay, fishermen catch largemouth bass, catfish, and pike. Further down the Chesapeake, bottom fishing with peelers and bloodworms, the sports fisherman goes after Norfolk spot, white and yellow perch, and small rock, or he casts or trolls with bucktails and spoons for larger rock. The marine mammals—porpoise, a stray whale, and harbor seals—find their way into the Bay. Besides the native turtles, sea turtles are occasional visitors.

Certain fish have been of particular importance and value in the Chesapeake's economy. In colonial times the shad was valued as a cheap but tasty food fish. The abundance and size of shad astonished the English;

111

fish a yard long were reported. In the spring runs, great quantities were seined from the Tidewater rivers. The catch has declined in this century, but shad still ranks second in value and fourth in poundage of the commercial finfish catch in Maryland. The peak catch of shad was made in 1890; the nets that year took about six times the average catch of recent years.

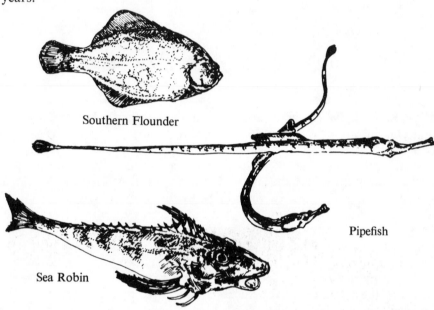

Southern Flounder

Pipefish

Sea Robin

Shad are of the herring family and, herring-like, have large scales, a deep, compressed body, and a large mouth. The female, or roe shad, is larger than the male, or buck; the fish average three and four pounds respectively. The shad is anadromous. It is believed, but has not been conclusively proved by tagging, that shad return to the streams where they were hatched, presumably guided by odors distinctive to particular watersheds and streams. From March to May shad ascend the rivers in irregular waves, the males preceding the females. The fish congregate in shallow flats and upper tidal waters near the mouth of freshwater streams. The female produces up to one quarter of a million eggs; these sink to the bottom. The milt released into the water by the male fertilizes about two-thirds of the eggs. Shad make no nest for their eggs, and few of the fertilized eggs survive the natural hazards to become larvae or fry. The incubation period depends upon temperature and varies from three to six days. By the first winter, the survivors are eight inches long and are ready to leave the brackish estuaries for the sea, where they live for three to five years before their first spawning run.

In colonial times, most shad were taken by haul seine from the river banks. April, the month of the greatest runs, was the month of the largest catches. The pound net, a large trap with nets strung between stakes, and the gill nets, anchored, staked, and drifting, were introduced from New England after the Civil War. These nets produced much greater catches. Today the Potomac and Choptank rivers yield the greatest harvest by gill

Hardhead

Shad

net. Pound nets are a feature of the lower Bay. The value of the shad catch has declined from the peak yields of eighty years ago for various reasons. Overfishing, destruction or blocking of nursery areas by development, and pollution, in the form of acids from coal mines and sewage from cities, are assumed to be responsible. Recent studies in progress for five years have employed a number of techniques including sonic tags in an effort to reestablish the shad on the Susquehanna. A series of dams have kept the fish from spawning grounds. Shad do not ascend conventional fish ladders, but new designs of ladders and elevators are being studied.

The striped bass or rock is the most valuable fish in the Bay. While the striper ranges in schools all along the Atlantic coast, inshore estuaries and bays are its principal habitat and the Chesapeake its main nursery. Like the shad, rock are anadromous, living part of the time in salt water, part in fresh. From April through June schools enter the Tidewater rivers and migrate upstream until they reach fresh water. Before dams barred the way, striped bass traveled as far as 100 miles above the Susquehanna fall line. On the spawning grounds each female lays as many as five million spherical greenish eggs to be fertilized by the male. The adults return downriver leaving the eggs to hatch in about two days. The fry travel to the Bay where they grow rapidly on a plentiful supply of fish, crabs, and isopods. In summer the fish school near the surface of the open Bay. After moving inshore in autumn, they migrate toward the lower Chesapeake where they winter in deep holes. In the spring the cycle is repeated. Females make their first run upriver at about four years of age, males at two. One rock in ten swims to sea instead of the spawning gounds, often traveling as far north as New England.

Both sport and commercial fishermen prize the striper. The annual catch fluctuates but has increased steadily over the past 20 years to a value of over half a million dollars. In welcome contrast to the dwindling shad fishery, the rock catch has doubled since 1890. Commercial fishermen favor haul seines and pound nets but also set gill and fyke nets. Sportsmen land even more rock than commercial fishermen. Charter boats trolling the middle section in late fall make especially good catches. The stripers most often boated measure 14 to 18 inches in length. Growth rings on their scales show fish of this size range in age from three to eight years. Rock may live for 30 years reaching a weight of 120 pounds. Laws protect the larger fish because of their value as spawners.

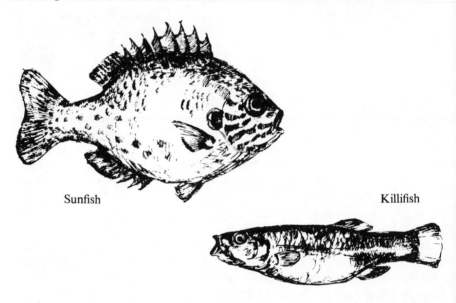

Sunfish   Killifish

Menhaden are caught by purse seiners in the lower Bay and outside the Virginia Capes. About fifty of these vessels, from eighty to one hundred and forty feet in length, operate from Chesapeake ports. These fish of the herring family are found along the East Coast as far north as Massachusetts. Though once considered good eating they are now caught for their oil and for fish meal, a feed for cattle and poultry. In recent years the catch of Atlantic menhaden has declined, in part, it is believed, because of overfishing.

Unlike shad and rock, menhaden spawn at sea. The larvae, transparent and ranging in size for $\frac{1}{8}''$ to $1\frac{1}{2}''$, enter the estuaries and congregate in large numbers in the Chesapeake's brackish tributaries. As the fish take on the general appearance of adults they cruise about in schools feeding on small crustaceans. The juveniles spend their first summer in the estuarine nursery; in the autumn, the schools begin moving out into the ocean. Juveniles and adults swim with mouths open, straining microscopic plants and animals. In general the fish are most abundant in the ocean near the mouths of bays and estuaries where the plankton are most numerous. Populations shift, however, and the menhaden recently have left the coasts above the Chesapeake. The reasons for their migrations are not clear.

Menhaden Purse Seiners

Although the catch of finfish has increased in Maryland waters, its value has not increased in proportion. Except for rock, the catch of valuable migrant species such as bluefish, croaker, and shad has fallen off. Rock catches have increased to the point that the market has been glutted when the fish come into the rivers to spawn. The finfisheries in Maryland have changed in the past two decades. There are fewer full-time fishermen; one-third of Maryland's commercial fishermen are seasonal or part-time. The trend has been toward cheaper gear involving smaller capital outlay, such as gill nets, rather than the pound nets or haul nets. The Director of the former Department of Chesapeake Bay Affairs, reporting on the condition of the finfisheries in 1968, predicted little increase in commercial production. Fewer migratory fish, changes in gear, fewer fishermen, competition with sports fishermen, and strict conservation laws such as that which outlaws the purse seine are all factors affecting the fisheries.

Virginia's fisheries suffer from similar problems. Young men and skilled workers are not attracted to fishing or the supporting industries of boatbuilding and seafood processing. The work in the boats is not easy compared with employment ashore. Handling a purse seine, haul net, or setting pound nets in all conditions of weather is rugged work. There has been relatively little mechanization or new gear in the last fifty years to ease the labor. In addition, prices, particularly of the less valuable fish such as herring and menhaden, have remained virtually the same for the last half century. Heavy imports from abroad and changing popular tastes have also hurt the industry. Today the per capita consumption of fishery products in the United States is relatively low, half that of England and one-sixth that of Japan. The result is "low and uncertain crew earnings," according to the Bureau of Commercial Fisheries in a report dated 1967. Despite an anticipated increase in demand as the country grows—it is expected that the Chesapeake will supply 466,000,000 pounds in 1980 and 664,000,000 pounds in the year 2000—the commercial fisheries, which reached the height of their growth eighty years ago, will continue to diminish in importance in the Chesapeake.

John Smith, observant as ever, noted:

> Of fish, we were best acquainted with sturgeon, grampus, Porpus, Seales, Stingrays whose tailes are very dangerous, Brettes, Mullets, White salmonds, Trowts, Soles, Plaice, Herrings, Conyfish, Rockfish, Eeles, Lampreyes, Catfish, Shades, Perch of three sorts, Crabs, Shrimps, Creveces, Oysters, Cocles, and Muscles. But the most strange fish is a small one like the picture of St. George his dragon, as possible can be, except his legs and wings: and the Tode fish which will swell till it be like to burst, when it commeth into the aire.

And in order to take advantage of the Bay's fish, Lord Baltimore wrote the following instructions to his colonists:

Provision for Fishing and Fowling

> *Imprimis,* necessities for a boate of 3. or 4. Tunne; as spikes, Nayles, Pitch, Tarre, Ocome, Canvis for a sayle, Ropes, Anchor, Iron for the Rither: Fishing-lines for Cod and Macrills; etc. Cod-hookes, and Macrill-hookes, a Seane or Basse-net, Herring-netts . . .

XIV

Shellfish

CHESAPEAKE, according to some translations, is the Indian word for "Great Shellfish Bay." The name is appropriate, for shellfish are the Chesapeake's pride. Marylanders and Virginians land half of the country's crab catch, and Maryland leads the states in oyster production. The Bay is a leading source of softshell clams, and landings of hardshells are on the increase. These, as well as a variety of less valuable crustaceans and mollusks, find in the Chesapeake an ideal combination of salinity, temperature, bottom composition, and food concentration.

Mud crabs, fiddler crabs, oyster crabs, and horseshoe crabs abound, but the blue crab is king of the crustaceans. Steamed crabs are the grand entrée of many a summer Tidewater menu, and crabcakes are a year-'round delicacy. Southern cookbooks are full of crab recipes—crab imperial, crab royal, crab salad, deviled crab, and a score of others. Sportsmen and sportswomen of all ages eagerly seek the blue crab for their tables, and the restaurateur's and housewife's purchases keep the crab fishery profitable.

Crabs spawn near the mouth of the Bay in Virginia waters; relatively few of the sponge crabs (females carrying eggs) are seen in Maryland. Juveniles migrate northward to feed and grow in the brackish creeks of the Tidewater. As must all animals with an exoskeleton, crabs shed or moult in order to grow. The local names for the various stages of the moulting process are green and ripe peeler, soft crab, and paper shell. Peelers are valued as fish bait or are kept until they shed. Defenseless soft crabs are easy prey for fish, waterfowl, or other crabs. They hide near the shoreline or, if females, are carried and protected by male crabs. Mating occurs while the female is soft; the pairs often seen swimming together in the middle of Bay are called doublers.

Crabs are taken by boxlike traps made of chicken wire, by trotlines baited with eel, or by individual lines baited with eel or chicken scraps and weighted with nails. The trotline may be as long as a mile; the crabbers

117

Rock Crab

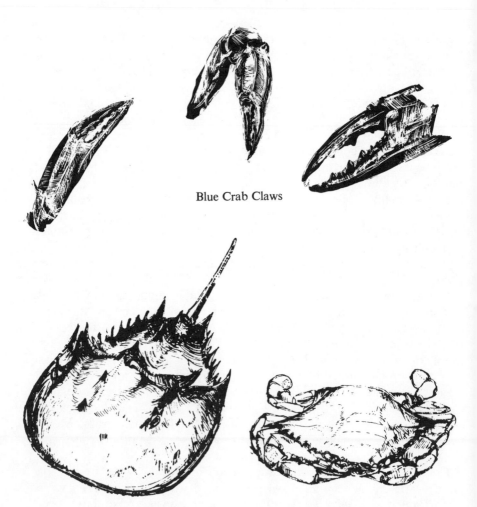

Blue Crab Claws

Horseshoe Crab   Blue Crab

row their skiff along the line, which passes over a beam secured athwart-ships and projecting over the side. As the line is lifted, one of the crabbers dips crabs while the other rows. The crabbers set their line before sunup and on good days find crabs on each bait. By eight o'clock the bait is gone, the bushel baskets are full, and the crabbers are heading for home. If there are no crabs, they coil their line, with baits attached, in a barrel of brine

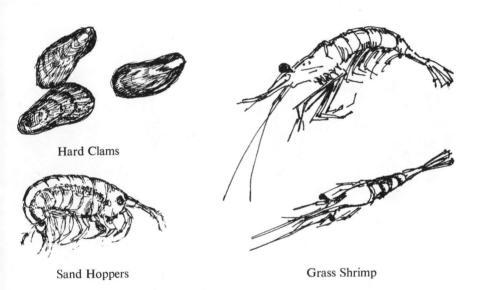

Hard Clams

Sand Hoppers   Grass Shrimp

for use the next day. The method may be mechanized somewhat with a patent catcher consisting of rollers and net rigged over the side of a power boat. Soft crabs are often caught by the solitary crabber standing in the bow of his skiff, poling himself around the stumps and old pilings near the shore. In summer the crab is caught on baited lines or netted while swimming. Virginia crabbers drag for them with dredges in winter while the crabs lie dormant in the soft sand.

Mud, fiddler, and oyster crabs are valueless commercially. Occasionally the horseshoe crab has been taken for pig food. The blue crab, on the other hand, normally leads the Maryland catch in weight landed and ranks second in value. The catch fluctuates radically. Record landings in 1965 and 1966 were followed in 1968 by the lowest of the century. Changes appear to result from conditions of water temperature and salinity. Despite Maryland's criticism of winter dredging and taking sponge crabs by Virginia, heavy catches do not appear detrimental. Since crabs live no longer than two or three years, few would survive even if they were not

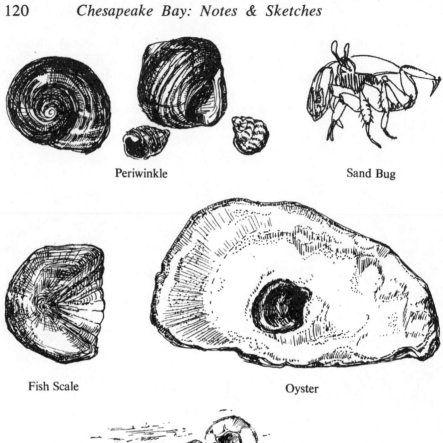

Periwinkle

Sand Bug

Fish Scale

Oyster

Barnacles

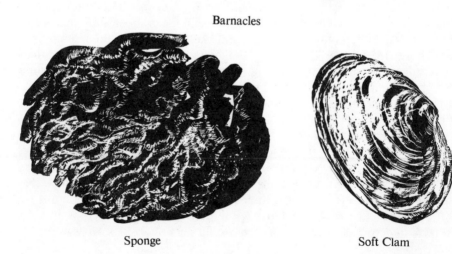

Sponge

Soft Clam

caught. Crabs often come back in great numbers after a particularly bad year. It appears, in fact, that a smaller stock of spawning crabs produces a larger number of progeny.

Another crustacean, the grass or glass shrimp, is too small for the table but is excellent fish bait. Abundant in grassy shallows, they are easy to catch in a net with a roller on the bottom. Tiny crustaceans, isopods and copepods, are important as forage for large and small fish. One crustacean, the fish louse, turns the tables and lives in the fish's gills as a parasite.

The Chesapeake's mollusks include both valuable and destructive species. Among the latter is the shipworm or teredo, a pest well documented in Bay history. In colonial times ships were protected from its borings by a coating of pitch, lime, and tallow, by burning and scorching the bottoms, by frequent cleanings during worm season, and by mooring upriver in fresh water. George Washington reported that the Potomac at Mount Vernon was too fresh for shipworms, and Baltimoreans advertised the head of the Patapsco as wormfree. Some shipbuilders protected their hulls with sheathings of copper or of thin pine planks. Others relied on the "worm shoe," a pine strip laid on the bottom of the oak keel. According to their theory teredos do not cross the seam between the soft resinous pine and the hard white oak but remain in the worm shoe, sparing the keel. Some years were noted as bad worm years, when low rainfall raised salinity and allowed the teredo to invade normally fresh headwaters.

The shipworm seems to prefer some woods to others but none is immune. Entering the piling or boat timber as a larva, it matures in a cavity bored with its cutting shells. At one end of its thin elongated body are the foot and the shells; at the other, the siphons. As the name implies, the mature teredo resembles a worm more than a clam. Its shells make an efficient wood-boring bit enabling the shipworm to bore as much as four inches in a month. As the tunnels in a worm-infested timber do not penetrate the surface, the wood may appear sound. A probing knife blade, however, will reveal a network of cavities and a seriously weakened plank or keel.

The hardshell clam is found in the saltier lower Bay. Known farther north as quahog, cherrystone, or chowder clam, it is a close relative of the oyster. With its shell buried in the mud, the clam extends upward two tubes called siphons. Sucking water through the incurrent siphon, it extracts oxygen for respiration and plankton for food, then discharges it through the outcurrent siphon. Small clams can move over the bottom by extending the foot, expanding it to act as an anchor, then retracting it to drag along like a ship using a kedge. Larger clams, relatively immobile, can only move vertically up and down in the mud.

Clams are hermaphrodites, changing sex from one year to the next and spawning annually in June, July, and August. After a period as free swimmers, the larvae attach themselves by a thread to the bottom. From the thread develops the foot of the full-grown clam. Three quarters of an inch long after their first year, Bay clams grow faster than northern quahogs. Adults measure three to five inches in length. Clammers use the "shinne-cock" (a towed rake adapted from the quahog fishery), tongs, dredges, and various types of rakes. The simplest method, treading, requires no implements. One merely wades barefoot through the mud, finding and digging out clams with one's toes. Small clams are tastiest, raw or steamed, and command the highest price.

Razor Clam

Softshell clams, or "steamers," have become important commercially with the development of the hydraulic dredge. After its introduction in the 1950s production rose rapidly but has declined since 1964, partially because of a disease on the clam beds in the lower Bay. The dredging rig, mounted on a 40-foot deadrise workboat, includes conveyor belt, centrifugal pump, water jets, block and tackles, and two engines, one for the pump and one for the conveyor. Nozzles are secured to the forward end of the conveyor and connected to the pump by hoses. The crew lower the forward end to the bottom and adjust the after end to deck level. Starting the pump and belt, they steam slowly ahead. The water jets dig a trench in the bottom 30 inches wide by 18 inches deep, washing the mud to the conveyor. Mud and clams travel up the belt to the surface, where crewmen pick off legal clams, over two inches long, leaving the mud and undersize culls to fall back to the bottom. The heavy dredge, mounted on the starboard side, gives the boat a characteristic list. A few specialized catamarans have been built with the dredge hung between the two hulls. Hydraulic dredges are controversial. Critics charge that digging trenches and spreading silt tends to smother oysters and destroy other animal and plant life on the bottom. Some counties prohibit dredging, and it is banned on all oyster bars.

Certain Indian tribes on the shores of the Chesapeake subsisted largely on oysters, eating them raw and roasted and leaving great shell heaps at their village sites. The English settlers, while impressed with the size and abundance of the Bay's oysters, ate them only when other sources of food failed. During the Starving Time at Jamestown, one party of settlers went to an oyster bar at the mouth of the James and subsisted for weeks on oysters and a bit of Indian corn. Their survival points up one fact: oysters are nutritious. One could do worse than exist on an unbroken diet of oysters. Oysters were eventually taken commercially during colonial times

Hard Clams

and experiments were made for pickling them in various ways. Some appreciative colonists ate them stewed and frittered as well as raw and pickled. However, not until well into the 19th century was the oyster to come into its own.

Oysters, the colonists noted, were very large. They were variously said to be as large as a horse's hoof, four times the size of English oysters, thirteen inches in length, and so large they had to be cut in two before they could be swallowed. They were harvested then as they often are now, from a boat with a pair of wooden tongs; "below they are wide, tipped with iron." In 1793, Moreau de St. Méry wrote at Norfolk:

> Many boats engage in oyster fishing, using an iron scissors-shaped instrument ending in two rakes to scrape the oysters from the bottom of the river. The oysters are large but have little taste because the water is not sufficiently salty.

Oysters thrive in enclosed bays where salinity is reduced by fresh water entering from the rivers. The intermediate salinity of the middle portion of the Chesapeake is ideal. Starfish, an oyster predator, cannot live there. The nature of the bottom, rich plankton growth, temperature range, and the relative absence of pollution and sedimentation of this portion of the Bay also promote growth. Above Baltimore, low salinity and sediment from the Susquehanna have destroyed the oyster bars. Few Virginia waters, except certain stretches of tributary estuaries such as the lower James, produce oysters. Maryland is fortunate in having the most extensive beds.

The Chesapeake oyster is oviparous, releasing as many as 100 million eggs from one individual. Fertilization occurs in the water through the chance meeting with sperm. This haphazard approach to reproduction is compensated for by the tremendous numbers of eggs released. According to one set of calculations, five generations of descendants of one Maryland oyster would form a mass as big as five earths if half the eggs of each generation were fertilized, grew to maturity, and reproduced. In sum, the oyster has remarkable powers of reproduction.

After hatching, free-swimming oyster larvae or spats are scattered by the currents until they attach to some hard surface. Their place of attachment, the "clutch," permits them to continue development, but it also renders them immobile. Lacking a foot like the clam's, the oyster can never leave its clutch. If silt covers the bed or the environment becomes otherwise unsuitable, it must die. Eighteen gallons of water pass each day through the oyster's incurrent siphon, gills, and excurrent siphon. Millions of microorganisms stick to the mucus of the gills, providing the oyster's food supply, and the gill membranes exchange carbon dioxide for oxygen. The oyster has no brain and little sense perception. Gravity tells it which direction is up; it tastes the water passing through it; it can sense when it is touched. Beyond this limited sensitivity, it has no knowledge of the world outside its shell.

Oysters, according to William J. Cromie, of the Chesapeake Biological Laboratory at Solomons, are "better balanced from the point of view of nutrition than almost any other food. Whether raw or cooked their soft bodies contain essential vitamins and minerals, proteins of high nutritive value and starch in a readily digestible form." They are also low in calories. The months with the letter 'R', as almost everyone knows, are oyster months. Actually they may be eaten any month and some claim the Bay's oysters are at their prime in May and June, though other fanciers maintain that summer oysters are watery and tasteless. There is also greater danger in the summer of toxic bacteria and protozoans; infectious hepatitis can be contracted by eating oysters grown in waters polluted by sewage.

In 1875, 17 million bushels of oysters were dredged from the Chesapeake; in 1941, the Bay yielded seven million bushels. This reduction was due primarily to overfishing, though natural enemies and pollution have contributed to the depletion. The eggs and larvae are prey for a host of predators. Adults are attacked by starfish, boring snails, marine fungi, and the parasite *minchinia nelson* (MSX). MSX hit the Virginia beds in 1959, and the industry has yet to recover. Other hazards are storms which may bury the oysters in silt and mud. The mortality rate from natural causes has been estimated at 10 to 15 percent.

Despite the decline in production since the peak years of the 1880s when Virginia landed 45.4 million pounds and Maryland 70 million, Maryland still leads the country in oyster production. The 1968 catch brought $11,000,000. Oysters represent two-thirds of the value of Maryland's fisheries. Some bars yield as much as $400,000 in ten days of skipjack dredging.

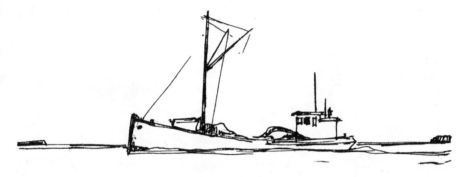

Oyster Buy Boat

Recognizing the value of this resource, Maryland has been spending $1⅓ million annually for the management of the oyster fisheries. The effort has succeeded in improving oyster production. Maryland generally has better conditions and more extensive grounds than Virginia with the exception of good natural seed beds. Maryland owns over 12 hundred acres of seed bed from which 1¼ million bushels of seed oysters are taken annually for seeding on the bars where spatfall is too light for maximum production. For each bushel harvested on a stocked bar, the state has invested about 60 cents in seeding. Another technique is spreading of clutch to which larvae attach themselves. Firms and individual oystermen have been employed to dredge clutch in areas no longer suitable for oysters, such as the grounds above Baltimore, and transport it to establish new bars elsewhere. It is sometimes charged that these efforts at management have failed, or have been influenced by political factors, but the programs plus relative freedom from oyster pests and blights have increased Maryland's landings in recent years.

Oysters are harvested by dredging and tonging. In Maryland dredging is done under sail except where the law has been modified to permit pushing with a yawl boat on certain weekdays. Skipjacks or dredge boats, V-bottomed sloops, and formerly, bugeyes and schooners, dredge in Maryland waters. The dredges are hauled aboard by donkey engines on deck; no engine for propulsion may be installed in the boat though all vessels carry yawl boats, usually powered by automobile engines, for pushing. The dredge boats are permitted to operate for a limited season, shorter

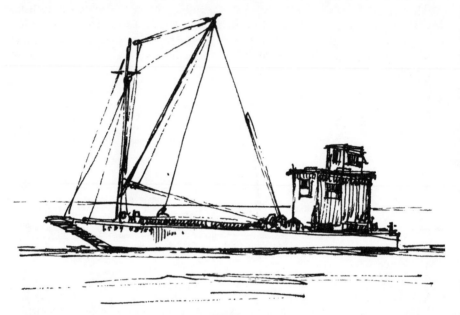

Barge

than that of the tongers, on specified bars. The number of boats dredging under sail is diminishing every year—the capital investment is high for a limited season that may be interrupted by weather. Upkeep of the boats is increasingly expensive and profits are uncertain. In towns such as Deal Island, at the southern end of Maryland's portion of the Bay, the industry has been hurt by MSX. Dredge boats are abandoned on the beach each year as costs mount and younger men turn their backs on the water. Between 60 and 70 boats now dredge whereas at the turn of the century, 1,000 worked the Bay.

Most tongers work from a deadrise, an open power workboat. Standing amidships, exposed to the elements, the oysterman works the long scissorslike poles until he feels the gathered oysters. He walks to the bow, lifts the tongs to the balance point, and swings the heavy rakes up and over the cockpit. Water, icy in winter, streams down the poles and up the sleeves. Dumping the rakes on the culling board, the waterman moves aft to sort the oysters. After knocking them apart, he throws overboard any culls under three inches. The law requires him to cull where he tongs so that under-sized oysters will be restored to the same bar. Dockside inspection and enforcement are rigorous.

Mechanization has eased the oysterman's life. Patent tongs, less stren-uous to operate, permit bigger hauls. Larger than hand tongs and lacking handles, they are lowered from a boom. On hitting the bottom they are tripped shut, sometimes by a special hydraulic system. A winch hoists the muddy load, and the boom swings it to the culling board. In cold winters, when freeze-ups close the rivers and Bay, powerful State of Maryland craft serve as icebreakers, clearing channels to assist the oysterman in his chilly work.

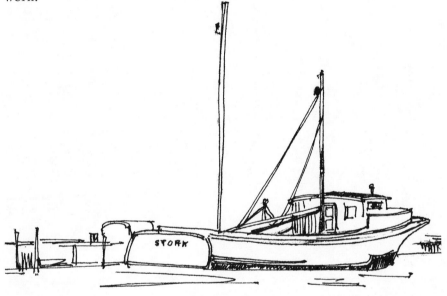

Patent Tonger

There are private as well as public oyster grounds in both Maryland and Virginia. Watermen dislike leasing of grounds, fearing a monopoly by large operators if the beds are closed to the public. The general feeling is that resources of the Chesapeake should be open to all on an equal basis. A man's right to oyster verges on being a natural right. In this spirit, a Marylander may tong in certain designated areas for his own use, taking up to a bushel each day of legal sized oysters without a license. Similarly, a man has the right to crab for himself without a license; he may run a trotline 100 yards in length. The waterman looks upon the Bay as a way of life and its resources as a gift of nature, a gift that has served men in the past and is well worth preserving for the future.

Boatyard on Eastern Shore

XV

Boats and Boatbuilding

IN NATURE, environment and natural selection work together in the evolution of species. Boat types, like natural organisms, also evolve in answer to local conditions. Whether the waters are calm or rough; whether the bottom is steep and rocky or sloping and sandy; what tasks are to be performed, what building materials are available—all these factors affect the design of boats in a given region during a given era. The Chesapeake, landlocked and narrow, is normally calm. The bottom is muddy and flat with extensive shallows. Commercial fishing, and in past years local shipping, have been the traditional tasks of Bay craft; pleasure boats now outnumber all others. For many decades, Bayside stands of oak and pine furnished cheap, high quality lumber for Chesapeake boatyards. Under these influences, Bay builders developed shallow draft workboats with low freeboard and ample deck space. Large sail areas were usual because of summer calms, but reef points were equally necessary to cope with autumn and winter squalls. Oceangoing craft slid down Chesapeake ways too; their designs reflected some local influences but were modified to provide for the needs of the high seas.

The oldest Bay design is the log canoe. The English colonists found the Indians making and using canoes—not the birchbark craft of the northern tribes but log dugouts. Lacking metal tools Indians would burn down a tree trunk and hollow it with fire and with stone implements. Colonial boatbuilders added two more logs fastened with drifts, and shaped them with saw, axe, and adze. Later canoes had bottoms of five logs; above the curve of the bilge their sides were planked. Builders worked by eye, with pegs to gage the thickness. They started the boats upside down, then righted them for completion. Details of construction varied with the locale and the materials available. Log construction was considered to take less skill than rib and plank or other methods, but it depended on a supply of suitable logs. The art has died out; no boats have been built in this way since the 1930s.

Skiff

Log Canoe

The few remaining canoes take two forms, working and racing, both rigged for sail. The Eastern Shore racing canoe carries a long sprit over clipper bow and carved trail boards. At the stern is an outrigger for the mizzen sheet block. She steps two masts, flexible and unstayed, with a club on each boom to increase sail area. To counteract the instability caused by her narrow beam, the crew climb over the side on hiking boards.

Log Canoe at St. Michaels

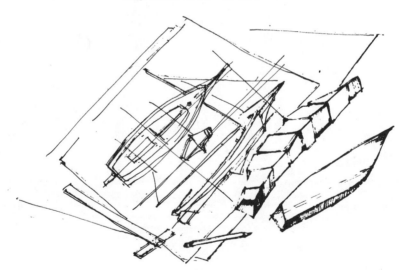

Half Models

Without this movable ballast a log canoe will capsize in still air when her sails are hoisted. Fast and beautifully turned out, the log canoe under sail is one of the most handsome craft in the Bay.

In her working rig the log canoe steps one or two masts and generally lacks a bowsprit and jib. A wider beam makes her more stable than the specialized racing canoe. In early versions the foremast was raked forward and carried a small leg-of-mutton head sail. Few working canoes still sail on the Bay; most are now in museums or rotting on mudbanks. Several years ago an old canoe was for sale for $250. She had formerly carried a small inboard engine. The engine, bed, and shaft had been removed, and a plug fitted the large hole cut in the sterm for a shaft log. Her two masts were unstayed, the main stepped well forward. Another one lies in the mud of Mill Creek off Whitehall Bay. The charts used to show another up Back Creek. A third was found on the bank on Grace Creek on the Eastern Shore. Her remains lay in the woods, near the shore, where someone had dragged her after her last trip.

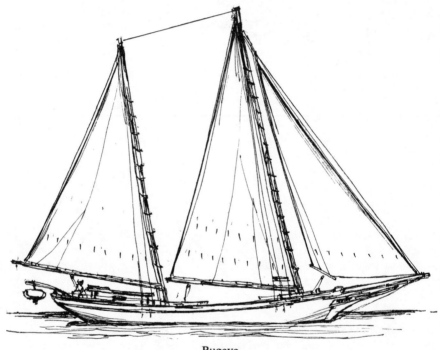

Bugeye

The colonists did not abandon conventional methods of boatbuilding when they borrowed and improved on the Indian dugout. The first recorded craft built in an American yard were a "Stout shallop," a "Frigot," and a "fishing boate," launched in 1612. In the next twenty years the settlers progressed to larger craft; Captain Henry Fleet used a 16-ton "barque" in 1632 to carry trade goods to the Indians. Two years later Captain William Claiborne set up a yard on Kent Island. Lacking roads, the expanding settlements needed watercraft for travel as well as for fishing. Yards soon developed at Baltimore, Taylor's Island, Oxford, and other Eastern Shore towns. Colonial Annapolis had a shipyard, ship chandlers, smiths who turned out ship fittings as well as horseshoes, and a rope walk.

The bugeye, double-ended and round-bottomed, evolved from the log canoe. Hulls were originally of log construction, and a few of this type are still afloat. Native to the Bay and found nowhere else, it was designed as an oyster dredger. Ketch rigged, the main mast is stepped forward of the shorter mizzen. She carries leg-of-mutton sails with a single large jib. In small bugeyes the masts are unstayed. A "patent" stern, somewhat like a pinkey's, extends aft of the rudder post in some boats. The added length makes the mast appear short and the boat under-rigged.

Two bugeyes still dredge with the Maryland oyster fleet. A few others are afloat as yachts or dude cruisers; one or two are preserved in museums. The rest are broken up or abandoned. The bugeye lacked the grace of the log canoe, pungy, and schooner, but it is sad that this unique craft has all but disappeared.

Schooners were developed early, both for Bay use and for the high seas. The oceangoing "Baltimore clipper" was apparently derived from a fast Bermuda design. Normally a schooner or a topsail schooner, the clipper was sometimes rigged as a brig with square sails on both masts. Fast sailers, they were a favorite of slavers, privateers, and other seafarers whose lives and fortunes hung on speed. The successful Baltimore design may have influenced the larger and more famous three-masted clippers built later in New York and New England.

Bay schooners shared the clipper bow of their seagoing sisters, but instead of a deep keel they featured shallow draft with a centerboard. Above the waterline they resembled the early New England fishing schooner before the introduction of the spoon bow. Similar craft sailed on Delaware Bay. A specialized schooner rig was the ram. Delaware built, the ram stepped three baldheaded masts in a slab-sided, flat-bottomed hull. The main mast was off-center to one side of the centerboard case. A donkey engine helped hoist the sails with their heavy gaffs, and a yawl boat pushed from astern when the wind died. Operating as freighters, they carried produce and bulk cargo as far north as Delaware Bay and as far south as Currituck Sound. Their beam and draft were set to let them through Great Bridge lock south of Norfolk in the Intracoastal Waterway, and through the old C. and D. Canal locks. A few operated outside the Virginia Capes in the Atlantic coastal trade. Small crews and negligible fuel costs allowed them to offer cheap freight rates, and they were able to compete with railroads and trucks until the late 1940s. Today one ram has ended as a cruise boat; another is disintegrating on a mud flat up the Wicomico River. The rest are gone.

Another two-master was the pungy. Like most Bay boats, she was beamy with shallow draft and full bows. A sharply raked stem, masts raked aft, and a broad dark stripe around the hull gave the pungy a handsome yacht-like appearance. Schooner rigged, the pungy influenced the design of fishing boats in northern states and in New England. As a sailing vessel, the pungy has probably disappeared from the Bay; a few may still operate under power. Gone too are the sharpie—used to taking oysters and terrapin—and the cat-rigged crab scraper.

After the Revolution, Bay shipyards produced some of the finest small warships in the new U.S. Navy. In 1799 a yard in St. Michaels launched the *U.S.S. Enterprise.* Displacing 135 tons and measuring 85 x 22 x 10 feet, she carried 12 six-pounders and a crew of 70. She served in three wars— the quasi-war with France in her first year, the Tripolitan Wars in the Mediterranean in 1801-1807, and the War of 1812. Stephen Decatur once commanded her, and she fought a famous two-ship duel, defeating *H.M.S. Boxer* off Portland, Maine in 1813. Bay craftsmen built her well; she was still on duty in 1823 when she stranded and broke up on Little Curacao in the Caribbean.

Trailboard

The last sailboats in the United States fishing fleet are the Bay's skipjacks. Developed in the 1880s for dredging oysters, the skipjack design has not changed. Nested at an Eastern Shore pier, a newcomer of the 1950s may lie alongside an eighty-year-old veteran; they are almost indistinguishable. The continued existence of the skipjack is a tribute to the skill of its designers and the workmanship of its builders, but those alone do not account for its survival. In a reversal of the usual rule, its inefficiency has saved it. As a conservation measure, Maryland authorities prohibit the use of power boats for dredging oysters. Their greater speed, power, and maneuverability would permit motorboats to exhaust the beds.

The skipjack is a V-bottomed centerboard sloop. The single mast is stepped far forward to provide a clear deck. The boom extends well over the stern. The mast is sharply raked and bowed aft as with so many Bay types, and a long bowsprit with trail boards adorns the clipper bow. The single jib is club footed. A complicated system of lazy jacks facilitates reefing. The rudder is outboard; beyond it extend davits for a yawl boat, the only propulsion engine permitted by Maryland law. A scuttle just abaft

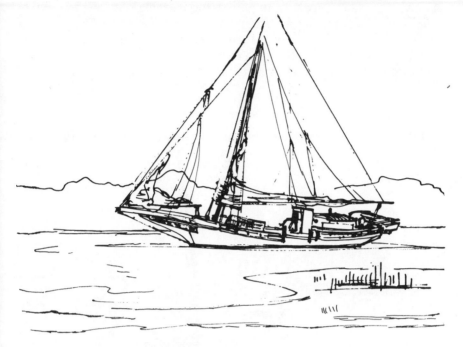

Skipjack on Eastern Shore Creek

Dredge Boats at Knapps Narrows

the mast provides access to the forecastle berthing. Aft of the scuttle is open deck for dumping and carrying oysters. A fence arrangement on each side keeps the piles of oysters aboard. Amidships is a large hold divided athwartships by the centerboard case. Abaft the hold is a house and a donkey engine for hoisting the dredge, then a deckhouse for captain

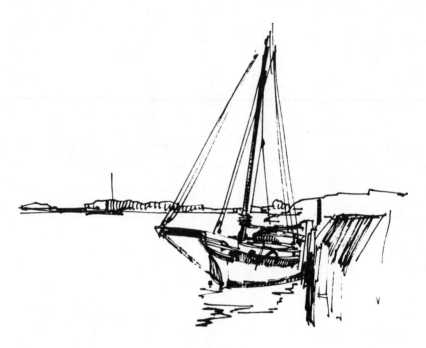

Dredge Boats

and mate. The wheel and horses for the main sheet perch on the stern. Rails, generally painted orange, follow the sides forward and aft of the break in the waist where the dredges are worked.

The boats need not be weatherly for dredging. They tack back and forth across the beds, often reefed, towing the dredge over the side. The beaminess and the hard chine provide the stiffness necessary for such work.

About 60 skipjacks work the beds for a limited season each fall and winter. For the rest of the year they are laid up at wharves and stakes along the Eastern Shore. Expenses go on even during the closed season: sails need repair, boats must be hauled for scraping and painting. Catches have diminished even under relaxed laws allowing the use of yawl boats for propulsion on certain days of the week. Considering the hard work and the small profit, it is not surprising that the fleet is shrinking. No new boats have joined the fleet since the '50s; it is doubtful that another working skipjack will ever be built. Used skipjacks come on the market from time to time; one can buy a boat with all its gear for less than $2,000. That is not much for a 45-footer.

Less colorful but more efficient, power craft perform the chores of yesterday's sailboats. The Bay has produced two distinctive designs, as

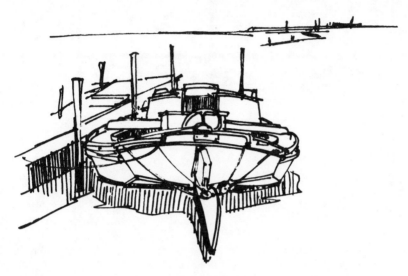

Chesapeake Deadrise

typical of the Chesapeake as the bugeye or the skipjack. The deadrise is a long narrow launch with a small house forward and a long open deck aft. Usually from 35 to 40 feet long, it has a shallow V bottom. There are two steering arrangements, a conventional wheel in the deckhouse and a

Older Power Yacht

vertical pivoted lever in the waist coupled to the steering cables. From the after position one man alone can control the boat while he works his trotline or crab pots.

The other design is the Hooper Islander. An exception to the rule of efficiency, her hull's distinctive shape is the result of prejudice or taste

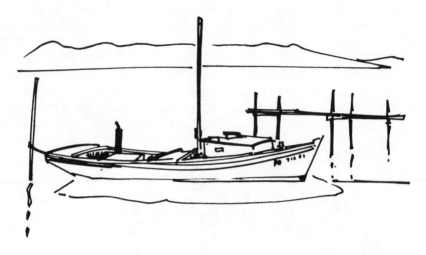

Deadrise Rigged for Patent Tonging

Ketch

rather than science or utility. The Hooper Islander has an unusual stern, a duck-tailed affair, expensive and complicated to build, and with no advantages in tonging oysters. It is apparently an imitation of the stern of early high-speed Navy torpedo-boat destroyers that once operated off Hooper Island. In those larger, faster craft the unusual shape prevented the stern from squatting at maximum speed; in the Hooper Islander it seems to contribute nothing except satisfaction to the eye. The rest of the boat is conventional; her hull is long and narrow with a V bottom. A small house forward provides primitive accommodations. Like the deadrise and all other Bay workboats, she is painted white.

Sloop

The Chesapeake has contributed its share of the world's interesting boat types. One might expect some of the designs to have survived as yachts, but few have made that transition. The large rams and schooners were either too roughly built to attract the yachtsman or else had disappeared before anyone with money took a fancy to them. The smaller types make poor yachts because of their shallow V or flat bottoms. To provide a cabin with any headroom, one must build a high, unsightly deckhouse that destroys the clean low lines of the workboat and makes an unweatherly design even less handy. They make satisfactory day sailers, and a few sail the Bay as weekend cruisers. But basically they developed as workboats and workboats they will remain.

One Sunday off Greenbury Point a skipjack was beating up the Bay past a fleet of sloops racing dead downwind toward the finish line. Round bottoms, fiberglass, and multicolored nylon spinnakers set the sloops an

Spinnakers

era apart from the workboat with her battered wooden topsides and her patched canvas. The sloops were beautiful—light, fast, racing machines, lovely to look at and exciting to handle. But it was the skipjack that captured the true spirit of the Bay—the skill of Chesapeake craftsmen, the hardiness of the watermen, the abundance of its resources, its pervading sense of history. She tacked and settled on a long beat toward Kent Island, slow and heavy, clumsy but durable. Long may she sail.

XVI

War Between the States

POLITICALLY and strategically the waterways dominated northern Virginia, the cockpit of the Civil War. The Potomac divided the Union from the Confederacy, and the Chesapeake not only isolated Virginia's Eastern Shore counties but also flanked the state on the east. The Tidewater rivers extended Federal naval power far inland, protecting Washington and threatening Richmond. In Union hands the waterways provided a safe supply line for their drive on the Confederate capital and severely restricted movement of southern land forces. Outgunned and outnumbered, the Confederate navy could not hope to command the rivers and Bay but did its best to harass the Union fleet.

Except for the campaign to deny the rivers to the Federals, Confederate action on the water was limited to raids and feints. Although colorful, daringly executed, and appealing to the romantic tastes of the times, these raids were of little significance compared to the struggle to control the rivers. The Union navy commanded the Chesapeake throughout the war. Only once did control of the Bay slip toward the Confederates when the powerful ironclad *Virginia* (ex-*Merrimack*) menaced the Federal fleet. The North feared and the South hoped that this ship alone could sweep the United States Navy from the waters of the Chesapeake and ascend the Potomac to attack Washington itself. The timely arrival of the *Monitor*, a ship of even more radical design, countered the threat of the *Virginia*. In the end, the *Virginia* was destroyed by her own crew as the Union army advanced up the James.

The Confederates briefly established a blockade (as they pridefully called it) of Washington. To the embarrassment of the Federal government and its navy, artillery of the Virginia state navy and militia took command of the Potomac at Aquia Creek and Mathias Point, not far below Washington. Batteries on the Virginia shore closed the river to commercial shipping and made it hot for passing naval vessels. From Aquia Creek a small steamer supported the artillery, taunting the Union navy by occasional sorties into the Potomac. From May 1861 until March 1862, the Virginians boasted, no ships passed except a few schooners not worth the shells to sink them. An irate Northern press demanded immediate elimination of this affront to the dignity and prestige of the nation's capital, but more serious was the effect on the logistics of the Federal forces

Lower Potomac Shore

around Washington. Supplies for the Army of the Potomac reached Baltimore by water where an average of 60 ships unloaded daily. Dock laborers shifted the cargo to wagons and railcars. To supply the 200,000 soldiers and Washington's swelling civilian population required 400 railroad cars on the one-track B and O plus a train of 100 horse-drawn wagons.

On May 31, 1861, the Federals began their campaign to open the river. The three steamers of the Potomac Flotilla fired over 800 shells at the Aquia Creek earthworks, but the only casualties admitted by the Confederates were one artilleryman's finger and a few yards of railway track. Next, the Virginians contrived to build a secret earthwork at Evansport. Although the Potomac was a mile and a half wide, the channel swung close to the Virginia shore. Working out of sight behind a riverside pine grove, the Confederates emplaced 20 guns including a British Armstrong

135-pound rifle brought by way of Bermuda. With the battery completed, the artillerymen cut half through each pine trunk to permit quick unmasking of the guns on approach of a target. Unfortunately for them, a strong wind toppled the weakened trees and disclosed the ruse. A passing warship discovered the fresh earthworks, and the next day the steam sloop-of-war *Seminole* engaged the battery. A Union officer described the battle in a dispatch to a Northern newspaper:

> They sent us at least thirty rifled shells and balls, all splendidly aimed, their guns being evidently well manned. Some of their shot and shell went over us, about eight or nine feet clear of the decks, and only a few feet above my head . . . Some burst just outside, before reaching us, and some just over our heads. Fragments of shell flew about the deck, and splinters in thousands.
>
> We were struck eleven times . . . How the shells do hiss and the shells sing aloud—a perfect distinct, fascinating locust-like song.

The naval gunfire did little damage, however, nor did future bombardments. It was Federal pressure on Richmond, threatening the rear of the shore batteries, that finally caused their abandonment and reopened the Potomac.

In June, 1861 there occurred one of those episodes so dear to those who like dash and melodrama in military exploits. The *St. Nicholas,* side-wheel steamer, was captured at the mouth of the Potomac by a group of Confederates disguised as passengers, who had boarded the vessel in Baltimore. The young commander of the hijackers, Colonel Thomas, was said to be of a good and ancient family of southern Maryland. He disguised himself as a middle-aged Frenchwoman and, according to the story, engaged the unsuspecting Federal officers aboard the ship in animated, accented conversation. At the proper moment he retired to his cabin and, as one of his men related:

> We all knew that the time for action had now arrived, and we gathered together awaiting the reappearance of Thomas. It was but a few minutes when, with a shout, he sprang from the state-room in the dress of a Zouave, armed with cutlass and pistol. The balance of us made a rush to the state-room, where our arms were concealed, and likewise secured pistols and cutlasses. In a few minutes we overpowered passengers and crew, secured them below the hatches, and the boat was ours.

We are told that the lady passengers were treated "without a single act of rudeness," and that the commander assured them that "they were in the hands of Southern gentlemen, and would be treated as their own sisters." The ship was taken to the Virginia shore, the plan being to load it immediately with a company of troops, Tennesseans with steamboat experience, and head up the Potomac to board the ships of the Federal Potomac Flotilla. It was assumed the familiar *St. Nicholas* could easily get alongside the northern ships without challenge. The troops were not ready, however, and since the timing was crucial, the plan was aborted.

Col. Thomas became the toast of Richmond; for a time he was much in demand to re-enact his role as a French lady. Eventually he assumed the nom-de-guerre of "Zarvona" and was later caught by the Federal military police attempting to capture another Bay steamer, the *Martha Washington*. He languished in prison for two years before being exchanged and, to the surprise and disappointment of his fans, retired from active military service.

Harassing the enemy in any way possible, Southerners put out the lights at Cape Henry and Cape Charles and all those on the seaward side of Hampton Roads. A guard from the *Cumberland*, sloop-of-war, kept the Willoughby Spit lightship in operation until, as a Richmond paper reported, "a party of gentlemen organized under the act of Congress for the creation of a volunteer navy" boarded and captured the light ship and took it to the Great Wicomico River. She was re-captured by an armed steamer sent out by General Butler, the general-politician who was then military governor of Norfolk.

Southerners, sometimes men home on leave from the Army, occasionally went on privateering expeditions on the Bay. One young officer, Acting Master John Yates Beall, set out to make himself the "Mosby of the Chesapeake." With 20 men operating in open boats, he aimed to "burn light houses, sever submarine cables, capture transports and steamers, and otherwise harass the enemy." In August, 1863, he made a wreck of the lighthouse at Cape Charles. He took five schooners before being captured by an armed flotilla sent out by the Federal commander of the Eastern Shore. The Federal authorities considered trying Beall for piracy, but dropped the charge after Confederates threatened reprisals against Federal naval prisoners of war.

Grimmer and more important struggles affected the fate of armies on the James River. In May 1862, Federal ships attempted to accomplish what McClellan was cautiously driving for in his Peninsula Campaign. Three ironclads, including the *Monitor*, tried to force the James River to Richmond. At Drewry's Bluff, seven miles below the city, the defenders sank obstructions and drove pilings to force ships to pass close under the guns of the batteries commanding the river. The guns were manned by army artillerymen and men of the Confederate Navy, some from the scuttled *Virginia*.

The Federal vessels silenced or passed the lower batteries and engaged those at Drewry's Bluff. Had they begun their assault immediately after the *Virginia* had been destroyed and before the defenses had been completed, they might have succeeded. As the ships approached, army and marine sharpshooters opened fire from the banks. The *Galena*, deliberate and seamanlike, ignored heavy fire from the shore batteries and anchored directly before them. An appreciative Confederate wrote:

> The attack on the part of the *Galena*, I think, was one of the most masterly pieces of seamanship of the whole war. She was brought into action in the coolest manner; indeed, she was brought to and sprung across the channel in a much more masterly way than I have often seen at mere target practice. She steamed up to within 700 or 800 yards of the Bluff, let go her starboard anchor, ran out the chains, put her head in shore, backed astern, let go her stern anchor from the starboard quarter, hove ahead, and made ready for action before firing a gun.

Despite this skill, the attempt was a failure. The *Galena* took a heavy battering while firing 283 shot and shell herself. After fighting all morning, the Union vessels fell back downstream and abandoned their effort to force the river to the Confederate capital.

The Confederates built a naval force on the James above Drewry's Bluff. The most powerful was the *Richmond*, a heavily armored ironclad. This force made one sortie down the river but was stopped by obstructions placed, this time, by Union forces. It is remarkable that the more powerful Federal forces should resort to closing the river, normally a defensive move.

Confederates began mining the James in 1863. These moored "torpedoes" were electrically detonated from rifle pits in the banks. In May 1864 the gunboat *Commodore Jones* was blown up; the next day, the *Shawsheen* was destroyed. The Federals were then lucky enough to capture a member of the Confederate Submarine Battery Service, and with a trick old as war itself, placed the prisoner in the lead minesweep. He told all he knew about the mines in the James. Within a month, twenty mines were swept, one holding 1,900 pounds of powder.

During the long, costly months of Grant's siege of Richmond and Petersburg, the Federal forces on the James tried to bypass the Confederate river defenses by cutting a canal through a loop in the river at Dutch Gap. Thousands of men dug, sometimes under fire. Two blasts finally opened the cut and the river streamed through, but Federal ships never used the canal. Richmond was captured when the exhausted Confederate Army retired before the overwhelming power of Grant. The men of the Confederate Navy on the James destroyed their ships for the final retreat toward Appomattox.

XVII

Point Lookout, Prisoner of War Camp

POINT LOOKOUT State Park is popular with campers from Washington, Baltimore, and Richmond. Swimming, crabbing, and bird watching are excellent, and there is a fine, open view of the sweep of the Potomac as it joins the Bay. In summer on Friday afternoons the campgrounds fill with hundreds of trailers, campers, and tents. A very different kind of tent city covered Point Lookout in 1864, a Federal prisoner of war camp.

Several miles from the park itself is a small fenced area enclosing some monuments, the largest reaching high above the surrounding loblolly forests. These mark the common grave of the prisoners who died at the camp. Only their skulls are buried beneath the monument; they were moved there after the war from the prison burial ground (known to the prisoners as the Peach Orchard). At the base of the main column bronze plaques list the names.

A causeway with the Bay on the left and a saltwater pond on the right leads to Point Lookout itself. The road passes a grove of tall pines, the dead ones with osprey nests, and then leads to an historical marker. On Point Lookout, it says, twenty thousand Confederate military prisoners and civilian sympathizers were imprisoned. Over three thousand died.

President Lincoln in March 1861 swore an oath to uphold the constitution and laws of a union that was disintegrating. Some states had seceded, other states were to follow shortly, and still more appeared bent on the same course. Maryland was a border state. The riots in Baltimore, the Southern sympathies of many Marylanders, the location of the capital of the Union, and the war potential of the resources of the state all made it urgent that Maryland be held for the Union. Force and arbitrary power were not spared by the Federal authorities to secure Maryland. The legislature was dismissed, habeus corpus suspended, the martial law imposed. Some of the civilians imprisoned by the military authorities were later sent to Point Lookout. Civilians were a minority of the prisoners, however; most were soldiers who began arriving after the Gettysburg campaign.

The Federal army leased the Point for a hospital in 1862. Before the War, Point Lookout had been a regular stop for Bay steamboats and

vacationers who patronized its resort hotel. The Point was strategically
located for an army hospital; it was easily reached by water from important
theaters of operations up the Potomac, Rappahannock, or on the Peninsula. Supply was no problem since Federal shipping from Baltimore
passed in a continuous stream. The hospital was a large wooden structure
built on a radial plan often used in Civil War hospitals. Steamers docked
at a long wharf on the Potomac side. The only problem was the inade-
quacy of the water supply on the sandy point. Its various advantages
made it a logical site for a prison camp; additionally, it was virtually an
island. From the point of view of the prisoners, however, it was a hell.

Point Lookout

Camp Hoffman, as the prison was officially called, was a compound of
26 acres surrounded by a 12-foot board fence. On a catwalk on the outside,
guards patrolled all hours of the day. Inside the palisade, a ditch marked
the deadline, so called because a prisoner crossing it would be shot without warning. Except for utility and administration buildings inside the
compound, shelters were army tents, many torn and rotten. Prisoners
suffered severely from exposure as winter rains and winds and freezing
weather swept across the low, exposed point. The men built fireplaces in
the tents, but there was never enough wood for warmth and cooking.
Clothing issues were few and far between; prisoners went barefoot summer

and winter. According to one, blankets were in such short supply that three men shared a blanket in the freezing tents. Crowding and dirt added to the general misery.

Food was poor in quality and short in quantity. For a time a few prisoners received packages from friends and from an organization in Baltimore that tried to ease the lot of the prisoners. Some of the men did odd jobs or made things to sell or traded to supplement their rations. Water came from shallow wells and, according to Army medical reports, was unfit to drink. Later, limited quantities of drinking water were brought in by ship; the water shortage contributed to the dirt and unhealthiness of the camp. Medical and hospital facilities were as limited as the other necessities. The poor condition of the men made them vulnerable to disease, and smallpox epidemics swept through the crowded camp.

One is led to comparisons with the notorious Southern camp at Andersonville. Photographs of Andersonville taken from the catwalk show a deadline made of a rail set on posts. The Confederates provided no shelter at all and the men were forced to burrow into the ground. The crowding was such that the hovels were built right up to the deadline. The weather was milder than on Point Lookout and the lack of clothing was not such a severe hardship. Water was more plentiful because a stream, though fouled, ran through the camp. The photographs of prisoners exchanged from Andersonville and taken to the military hospital at Annapolis, Maryland, show starved men. The South had fewer resources than the North to expend on the care of prisoners, particularly toward the end. In both North and South, the state of the camps was the result of callousness, bureaucratic indifference or inertia. The armies' overriding concern was fighting the war.

Medical teams inspecting Point Lookout reported the desperate state of affairs. Action on these reports, if any was taken, was invariably minimal or long-delayed. The conditions were brought to the attention of men high in the Federal government, but there was little interest. One dismissed the report with the observation that military prisoners were used to living in tents under rough conditions. At times a policy of calculated mistreatment prevailed. General Ben "Beast" Butler, then in charge of military prisons, was as harsh and vindictive as he had been when military governor of New Orleans and Norfolk and was to be later as Radical Republican leader in Congress after the war. Butler ordered deprivations as a reprisal for mistreatment and neglect of Federal prisoners in Southern camps.

Butler restricted the sending of parcels to prisoners and forbade visits by relatives and friends of prisoners unless the visitor secured a pass signed by the Secretary of War. Butler also ordered that one-third of the guards be Negro troops. The Southern prisoners resented the assignment of Negro guards, who, they claimed, deliberately humiliated and mistreated them. A set of drawings made by a prisoner shows men being forced to dance barefoot on the frozen ground while the guards in warm capes pointed pistols at their feet. Others claimed the Negro guards forced the men to pray on their knees for President Lincoln and the Northern cause. There were several cases of prisoners being shot out of hand by guards.

Light at Point Lookout

White guards shared in the brutal treatment. One Southerner wrote of his arrival by steamer at Point Lookout. The prisoners were formed on the dock for inspection. Any gear or clothing marked U.S. was kicked into the Potomac. The loss was serious for the prisoner generally had to rely solely on what he carried into the camp with him. For over a year, no clothing or shoes were issued.

The camp was protected by three earthwork forts. Picket boats patrolled the river and Bay. Two Southern plans were made to liberate the prisoners. In one, a ship loaded with arms was to make a dash into the Bay to Point Lookout. The armed prisoners would then break out into southern Maryland, where, with a sympathetic populace, they would present a serious threat behind the Union lines. This plan failed when the ship carrying the weapons was wrecked in North Carolina waters. In 1864 General Jubal Early planned to liberate the prisoners during his raid into Maryland, where they would join him for the attack on Washington. He detached General Johnson with a column to march to Point Lookout. A reconnaissance of the capital's defenses, however, discouraged Early. He recalled Johnson and returned to Virginia.

It was the Union victory that finally freed the prisoners. An old lithograph portrays the scene. Guards are marching a line of prisoners to an orderly room where they will take the oath of allegiance and be paroled. The Federal officers, spruce and healthy behind their desks, make a sharp contrast to the wretched rank of scarecrows. So ended the war at Point Lookout.

One wall of the fort remains; a century's rains and tides have destroyed the others. Inside the square of the fort a few vine-covered mounds of earth mark the old gun platforms. A lucky visitor, digging in the sand, may turn up a minié ball or a tarnished brass buckle. Little else at Point Lookout remains as a reminder of the strife and misery of the War Between the States.

XVIII

Pollution and the Chesapeake
The Nature of the Problem

IN THE BIOSPHERE, that thin shell surrounding the globe where life is found, many cycles operate to maintain a relatively constant environment. Animals, plants, radiant energy from the sun, ocean currents, and other inputs and forces, in fact all matter, play a greater or smaller part in this ecosystem. There are many cycles, infinitely interrelated. Some are an uncomplicated and humble series of events while others are as grand as the solar system.

Change is the unvarying characteristic of life and nature. The changes we are accustomed to seeing in the Chesapeake, however, are gradual or are part of a recurring phenomenon. All the species in the Bay have life cycles related to seasonal changes, the cycle of day and night, or life cycles of other species. The rock and the shad migrate up and down the Bay; others migrate vertically from bottom to surface and then down again in the course of a day. Different species are related in food webs and chains, and their numbers vary in relation to each other. The physical and chemical environment is constantly changing. The tides rise and fall. Water cycles between the Bay, the sky, and the land that drains into the Bay. Nitrogen and other elements cycle through the atmosphere, microorganisms, plants, and animals. All life depends upon the maintenance of certain concentrations. Fresh surface water enters the Bay from rivers and flows down the Chesapeake, while the more saline, deeper waters circulate to the head of the Bay. These are but a few of the multitude of complex, interrelated processes that operate continuously in the Chesapeake.

The concept of a constant environment is relative. In nature there is always change, but the rate varies. In communities of a number of species, a certain species dominates for a period. This plant or animal, like everything else that lives, changes the ambient conditions and, in time, makes the environment less favorable for itself. Thus it prepares the way for the

153

dominance of another species that can better exploit the new conditions. The former dominant species does not become extinct, generally, but takes a less conspicuous place in the community. The rate of change may be rapid until a new state of relative equilibrium is reached.

Man participates in these relationships. He may live in harmony with the plant and animal community, disturbing it but little, or he may change it radically. Primitive man lives in close harmony with nature and causes

Dorchester Marsh

few changes. As his society evolves, however, and advances technologically, his ability to alter the environment increases. In an advanced, industrialized culture, man employs machinery and chemicals that enable him to alter the environment rapidly. He simplifies ecosystems to serve his temporary convenience. The complex systems in nature, as it happens, are more flexible and safer for life; many alternate paths are possible. The changes man has produced have been fatal to many species and, in the end, may be so for himself. Hopefully man, with advanced technologies, can learn to live without upsetting nature. If he cannot, he will continue to poison the environment for himself and other living things. The question now is how much of the waste of industrial society can be absorbed and assimilated by the natural environment. The tolerance of the cycles that keep the conditions of the atmosphere, land, and waters relatively constant are as yet unknown.

Man's use of the Chesapeake introduces powerful new elements. Recreation, harvesting fish and shellfish, cultivating the lands that drain into the Bay, attempts to control the insect pests, fertilizing the soil, dumping of human and industrial wastes, all these lead to change. His activities affect the temperature of the Chesapeake, and he alters the depth and shape of the shoreline. In small amounts the natural system can tolerate all these.

The Patuxent River has become a hostile environment for ten species of fish formerly native. Heat pollution and low oxygen concentrations caused by bacteria living on the nutrients from treated sewage have killed them. Future plans call for dumping ten times as much sewage into the river. Since there are no plans for the recovery of nutrients, the situation can be expected to worsen. Washington releases eight million pounds of nitrogen into the Potomac each year; this amount will probably double in the next thirty years. The Potomac estuary is damaged now; what is to come?

Chesapeake recreation is on the increase. In a recent six-year period, the number of boat registrations increased by one-third. Approximately 120,000 boats are registered in Maryland and Virginia, and perhaps another 40,000 are unregistered. Large numbers of boats enter the Bay from

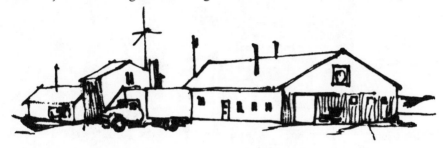

Processing Plant on Eastern Shore

other states; the grand total may be as many as one quarter of a million boats using the waters of the Chesapeake. Some 600 docks and marinas serve this fleet. Considerable local pollution results from marine toilets, and possible harmful effects of underwater exhaust of thousands of outboard motors are not yet known.

Chemical pollution from industry is controlled by state and federal law. Except for local conditions in Norfolk and Baltimore harbors, it is not a serious threat. Accidental oil pollution from ships occasionally occurs, however. Potentially dangerous pollutants are the insecticides carried into the Bay in runoff. Most of these were used for insect control in agriculture; spraying for mosquito control is another source of pollution. The effects of these agents on the life of the Bay are gradually becoming known.

The indiscriminate use of DDT illustrates the dangers. DDT is a "hard" pesticide, meaning that it decomposes chemically very slowly. Its half life is ten years, and it accumulates to poison the environment. Fish are particularly vulnerable when pesticides enter the water from runoff and contaminate the food they eat. The pesticides accumulate in even higher concentrations in animals, including man, who eat fish. The National Audubon Society was told at its 64th annual convention that the American eagle will become extinct unless DDT is banned—the eagle's eggs are laid with thin shells; these break before they can hatch. Mallard ducks are similarly affected. The effects of DDT on man are not known. There exist short-lived, soft pesticides that presumably are safer; these should be investigated.

Port of Baltimore

Thermal pollution means the raising of water temperature by industrial processes. Power companies have taken advantage of the Bay's large volumes of low-salinity water for cooling condensers. The number of power plants is increasing with the demand for electricity. In 1967, 22 plants were in operation or planned for the Bay or rivers leading into it. Some of these stations raise 1,000,000 gallons of water 10°–12° F. each minute. The largest of the plants will use 2,000,000 gallons. The accelerated demand for electrical power is characteristic of developed countries; the demand doubles every six to ten years in the Chesapeake region. This factor of thermal pollution will, therefore, become increasingly important.

The University of Maryland's Natural Resources Institute has concluded that heat pollution poses a danger to the entire Chesapeake. A six-year study of the Chalk Point station on the Patuxent revealed "a clear demonstration of some detriment" to the environment. This plant, not one of the largest, uses up to half a million gallons a minute. It raises water temperatures as far as five miles up and down stream. The state law limits discharge temperatures to 90° F., but at times Chalk Point exceeds this figure. Pollution, the study reports, destroys microscopic plant life passing through the condensers and therefore reduces photosynthesis in the river. It also notes damage to larger aquatic plants, mortality to crabs, oysters, and clams, and a general decline in fish population in the area. There was also metallic contamination in the surviving oysters in the river. On the other hand, certain shrimp are more abundant because of the heat, and in some respects the fishing in the immediate area was improved.

Temperature is known to be an important factor in the aquatic habitat; however, research in the field is not far advanced. Daily and seasonal behavior and the rates of biochemical reactions within the organisms are affected, but whether for good or ill is not always clear. Thermal pollution is lethal to some species, but may prove advantageous for others. Research and development may find useful applications for heat generated by power plants. One suggestion is to use it along with nutrients from sewage to culture algae for food. At our present state of knowledge, however, thermal pollution of the Bay seems to disturb the natural environment and should be controlled until its effects are known.

Nuclear power plants may eliminate pollution to air associated with burning coal and oil, but the risk of radiation may make it a dangerous substitute. Also the nuclear plant, like that burning fossil fuels, is a source of heat pollution. Two nuclear reactors are being built in the Calvert Cliffs to supply power for Baltimore. The plant will be built at a cost of one-third of a billion dollars. It is designed to generate more than 1.5 million kilowatts of electricity. Almost 2½ million gallons of water a minute will pass through its condensers; the differential in temperature between intake and discharge is ten degrees; the result, according to an advertisement in the papers, is the raising of the water temperature of 35 acres of the Bay three degrees. Present claims concerning the hazards of radiation conflict. Johns Hopkins scientists have testified that radiation from the plant could produce grave risks in the form of genetic deformities in humans. Tritium, the radioisotope released in the greatest amount, would "unquestionably bring a fractional increase in mutational damage." Experts for the project reply that safeguards would make the dangers to future generations infinitesimal. The Maryland departments of Health, Water Resources, and

Natural Resources have urged further research, a suggestion that could be wisely applied to many technological innovations.

Man changes the shoreline and depth of the Chesapeake to suit his various purposes. A 35-foot channel to Baltimore requires constant dredging. Shipping interests want a 45-foot channel. The fill from the dredging is dumped into spoil areas to the side of the channels where it creates shallows or, in some cases, dry land. Because of the value of real estate in harbors and, in the case of Washington, along rivers, there is pressure for filling operations to add acreage. Marshlands are drained and filled, and tributaries and rivers are dammed and channeled.

Increasingly, marshlands have been filled for development and for disposal of solid waste without concern for damage to life in the estuaries and Bay. Swamps and marshes are far from being unproductive, useless wastelands. Fish use them for spawning and nursery grounds, and waterfowl for resting places, feeding, and breeding grounds. For many forms of life, marshes are essential for the rearing of young. They are the habitat of the beaver, raccoon, and muskrat. The destruction of the wetlands would produce a lifeless Bay, with effects extending beyond the Chesapeake to the sea itself and to the summer breeding grounds of waterfowl thousands of miles away. Wetlands play a part in a larger scheme of life.

Recent plans call for filling marshes at Neabsco on the Potomac below Washington with compressed solid refuse from the city. One hundred and sixty acres of marsh would be covered first with a layer of trash and then with topsoil; the area would then be used for recreation. Neabsco points up the problem of solid waste disposal as an aspect of pollution. Washington, it is estimated, will produce over twice the solid waste in 1970 that it did 20 years before. Dumping into the water, burying in the ground, or burning the waste in each case loads the environment with pollutants. Rubber, metals, glass and plastics do not readily decompose or rot. Tires, for example, may be burned, in which case they pollute the atmosphere, or chopped up, which merely makes the rubber occupy less space. It has been suggested they be sunk at sea to form a series of barrier reefs off the Atlantic Coast. No other society has produced as much trash per capita as has ours. Like many of the pesticides and detergents, it is very hard to dispose of.

Statistics show a rapid acceleration of the developments that strain the Chesapeake environment. Our electrical needs double in less than one decade; the population in the area is expected to double in less than three. If we cannot control these developments, and we cannot, we must discover the effects these changes will bring. Lake Erie has become a biological desert. Timely action and a realization that technology destroys as well as achieves may prevent a similar tragedy in the Chesapeake.

XIX

The Effort to Conserve

UNDERSTANDING the Bay and its ecology is the key to its effective conservation. Institutions for scientific research have been studying the Chesapeake for over 40 years. Johns Hopkins' Chesapeake Bay Institute is a research division of the University's Department of Oceanography. Organized in 1949, the Institute operates a large, twin-hulled research vessel. At Gloucester Point are the Virginia Fisheries Institute and the Virginia Institute of Marine Science (VIMS), the latter affiliated with the College of William and Mary and the University of Virginia. VIMS operates several research vessels including a converted ferry boat, formerly on the Chincoteague Island run, and the *Pathfinder*, a modern, diesel-powered craft. Washington's Smithsonian Institution has interests in the Bay ranging from fossil studies at the excavations at Calvert Cliffs to research stations for the study of waterfowl.

A number of other Federal organizations are involved in Bay research. The Water Pollution Control Administration reports on the effects of pollution and the destruction of wetlands. Wildlife sanctuaries and management, particularly of waterfowl and game species, are the responsibility of the Fish and Wildlife Service. Special-purpose task forces include the group chartered by the government to study the Potomac river basin. Research, as well as construction and operations, concerns the Corps of Engineers.

Police, rangers, and wardens enforce conservation measures for Maryland's Department of Natural Resources, Virginia's Commission of Game and Inland Fisheries, and Maryland's Department of Water Resources. Baltimore's Port Authority has the task of managing one of the nation's busiest ports. The Potomac River Compact between Maryland and Virginia created a commission that provides for research, and regulating and licensing the fisheries of the Potomac. The Potomac River Basin Compact, signed by the District of Columbia, Pennsylvania, West Virginia, Maryland, and Virginia, is concerned chiefly with pollution control.

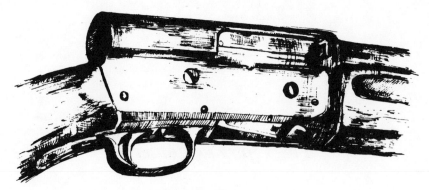

Browning Shotgun

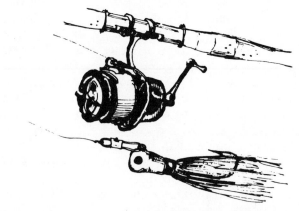

Bucktail and Spinning Gear

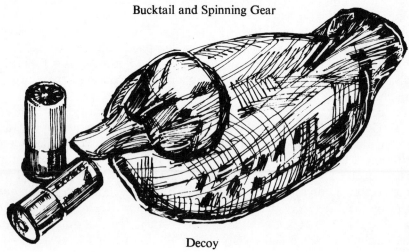

Decoy

The oldest of the research organizations concerned specifically with the Bay is the Chesapeake Biological Laboratory at Solomons, a division of the Natural Resources Institute of the University of Maryland. Thirty scientists on the staff conduct research centered on the ecology of estuarine life and extending into the chemical, physical, and geological nature of the estuary. The Laboratory maintains docks, boats, laboratories, and a museum. Thirty recent projects in progress included investigations of life histories of the oyster, the crab, and the rockfish; effects of thermal and other forms of pollution; taxonomy; and diseases of fish and shellfish. Discoveries at Solomons have led directly to better management of the Chesapeake's resources. The laboratories, for example, determined the optimum time to spread oyster clutch, and established a continuing record of commercial fish landings. The work ranges from the theoretical to the practical; technicians at Solomons first demonstrated the value of the crab pot.

The Corps of Engineers is designing a spectacular new research tool, the Chesapeake Bay Hydraulic Model. A smaller model of the lower James River has been used for the past two years to determine the effects of dredging on shellfish, the best location for sewage outfall, effects of outfall from conventional and atomic power plants, and the best location for fill projects. The Chesapeake as a whole faces similar problems. Though studies have been made by the Federal Government of the Potomac and Susquehanna as well as the James, the entire Bay has yet to be studied as a system. The model is designed for such an approach.

The State of Maryland has given land at Matapeake on the Eastern Shore for the project, which the Army Engineers will build, operate, and maintain. A replica of the Bay up to the fall line, the model will be of the fixed bed, geometrically distorted type, built to a scale of 1 to 1,000 horizontally and 1 to 100 vertically. The scale will allow a tidal cycle of 7.5 minutes or a year's simulation of tides in less than four days. The model itself will have an area of about six acres; the wetted area at low tide will be 166,000 square feet; at high tide, 184,000 square feet. The shore up to the 20-foot contour will be represented. Pumps and motorized valves will control the flow of water during the cycle. The model may be adjusted by altering the surface of the bottom to duplicate the tidal ranges, phases, and levels.

The model will aid the hydraulic engineer, water resource planner, and biologist. Fifteen different studies are awaiting the model's completion. These involve salinity distribution, mechanics of estuary flushing, effects of dredging, shoaling characteristics of the Bay and its tributaries, shore erosion, dispersal of oyster larvae by tides and currents, and environmental effects on control of parasites, jellyfish, and weeds. The model will be one of the most versatile tools available for system study and management of the Bay.

American Eagle

Through educational and public information programs, the state governments have sought to inform the public of the ecology of the Chesapeake and related problems of conservation. The Education Division of the Commission of Game and Inland Fisheries produces *Virginia Wildlife*, a monthly "dedicated to the conservation of Virginia's wildlife and related natural resources and the betterment of outdoor recreation in Virginia." Maryland's Department of Forests and Parks publishes *Oak Leaflets*, a series of pamphlets on the natural history of Maryland. The Department of Chesapeake Bay Affairs of Maryland produces *News Releases* and *Chesapeake Channels*, a publication rich in news on the Chesapeake but, unfortunately, with a limited circulation. The University of Maryland's Natural Resources Institute publishes a variety of pamphlets on the natural history of the Bay area. The Department of Natural Resources maintains a public information office that makes material available to schools and interested groups. Public school systems in Maryland are considering Bayorientated curricula and, over the years, more than 1,500 Maryland teachers have received courses at the Chesapeake Biological Laboratory. A private educational institution concerned with the life of the Tidewater is the Wye Institute in Maryland. This non-profit organization works with the people of the Eastern Shore to ease adjustment to the rapid changes as urbanization reaches the Bay. The Institute conducts experiments and demonstration programs in cooperation with public and private groups. Arousing public interest in the Chesapeake has also been the interest of certain business concerns whose advertisements promote the Bay country. The problem is large enough to welcome the attention of everyone who appreciates the Chesapeake.

It has been suggested that the Chesapeake be managed through a comprehensive federal organization like the Tennessee Valley Authority. Industry has traditionally opposed federal regulations against pollution. State laws have been relatively lax and poorly enforced, but state jurisdiction jealously protected. Actions of the federal bureaucracy, for its part, have not been uniformly consistent and efficient in the areas under its jurisdiction. Historically, industry and government have predicted prohibitive costs for effective pollution control. European experience, on the contrary, refutes the claim that industry cannot compete if it must clean up after itself or that a developed society must necessarily be a dirty one.

In September, 1968, the "Governor's Conference on Chesapeake Bay" met at Wye to consider the present state of the Bay and its future prospects. The goal was to formulate a course of action to conserve what the conference considered "Maryland's greatest natural resource." Papers covered various aspects of Chesapeake natural history, the threats posed by man's use and abuse of the Chesapeake, and suggestions for remedial action. A wide range of interests was represented: research, teaching, industry, government, and conservation. In terms of information exchanged and focus brought on the problems, the conference appears to have been a success.

Meetings like the Governor's Conference, effectively followed up, can create a program that will successfully conserve the Bay. The program must include continuing and increased research into the estuarine system and man's effect on it, organization to define problems and set goals, promotion of public interest and understanding, and establishment of finances and machinery to achieve these goals.

Index

165